Your Thrilling Future

Your Thrilling Future

Louis H. Evans, Sr.

Tyndale House Publishers, Inc.
Wheaton, Illinois

Scriptures in this book are from the King James Version of the Bible unless otherwise noted. Other versions used are *The Revised Standard Version of the Bible* (RSV), Copyright ©1952 by Division of Christian Education of the National Council of Churches of Christ in the United States of America; and *The Living Bible* (TLB), Copyright © 1971 by Tyndale House Publishers.

First Printing, May 1982
Library of Congress Catalog Card Number 81-85457
ISBN 0-8423-8573-8
Copyright © 1982 by Louis H. Evans, Sr.
All rights reserved
Printed in the United States of America

CONTENTS

ONE
The Long, Long Look
9

TWO
Death Is Universal
23

THREE
The Intermediate State
41

FOUR
The Resurrections
63

FIVE
The Judgments
75

SIX
Hell—The Abode of the Wicked
91

SEVEN
Heaven—The Final Home
109

PREFACE

Throughout my ministry, especially more recently, I have been encouraged by many to condense our Christian confidences about the future into a book. I have, in preparation, waded through many theories, speculations, and writings about Christian beliefs regarding the hereafter.

Many readers don't seem able to search through the libraries to examine the wealth of material on the details of prophecy, or to weigh the innumerable interpretations of the things that God has promised those who trust him.

Jesus said, "I go to prepare a place for you" (John 14:2). Since Jesus is the one who is preparing the place, he ought to know where it is. If our Christology is right, we believe all this concerning him and because we do, our future is secure and the information he has for obtaining eternal life is authoritative. Christ knew the glories of heaven, but he came to earth to give us the pattern, the power, and the program for tomorrow.

Christ said:

> I have yet many things to say to you, but you cannot bear them now. When the Spirit of truth comes, he will guide you into all the truth; for he will not speak on his own authority, but whatever he hears he will speak, and he will declare to you the things that are to come. He will glorify me, for he will take what is mine and declare it to you (John 16:12-14, RSV).

I hope this book will enable many to take a biblical glance at the five mountaintop experiences, and from the heights of Holy Writ scan the horizon of the Christian's tomorrow. Beyond this general scope, many may wish to search for further knowledge of the wonders of God's plan. Perhaps this book will be placed in the hands of inquiring friends and unbelievers to urge them to embrace the assurance of the future that is ours.

There will be some questions that are unanswered and different opinions and interpretations will swiftly be weighed. But when we search earnestly in the light of what God said about tomorrow, we may know that while God may not tell us enough to satisfy our curiosity, he has told us enough to satisfy our concerns.

1
THE LONG, LONG LOOK

WE HUMANS ARE THE ONLY CREATION OF God that shows the desire to look into the future. Being made in the image of eternal God, we have inherited the capacity to look toward eternal vistas. The question Job asked: "If a man die, shall he live again?" (14:14) is one only humans ask.

In driving an automobile, two views are necessary. The rearview mirror lets us see what is behind or where we have been. The human soul is constantly looking back from whence it came, what it has been doing. Memories of people and places still affect us. We learn from yesterday, and out of this consideration we shape our tomorrows. Through the rearview mirror we watch for traffic policemen, because of our fear of the consequences of breaking the law. But fear is legitimate, even if it is not the best motivation for careful driving. Spiritually it is wise to recall the folly of our sins and to seek forgiveness for them.

The backward glance reminds us also of God's favor. It reminds us of the progress we have made. We see the good deeds of ourselves and others that have left their tread marks of mercy behind us, the deeds that pleased God and ourselves.

Through the windshield we see the road before us. We look through it carefully to be aware of what is ahead: the white lines of God's guiding laws, the possible pitfalls, and all the signs that warn us of danger and move us to caution. Through the windshield we gaze expectantly ahead to enjoy the beauty before we actually see it. In this look ahead we also anticipate the fellowship of those who await us at the end of the way. We see how near we are to the pleasures and places which lie ahead.

So it is with the souls of people. A study of history may be enlightening, but it is never satisfying until we more than match it with a look at prophecy to see what is to be. This passion for new discoveries was placed by God in the heart of all of us.

Job's question is instinctive to all who are made in the image of God. "If a man die, shall he live again?" is one of the most universal inquiries we know today. About death there is no uncertainty—we all die, man and nature.

Botanically all life perishes. The grass withers and the flower fades and turns into loam and ashes. We might dry a beautiful flower and put it in its dryness behind a pane of glass to enjoy, but it is still dead.

Zoologically all animal life dies. One animal feasts upon another. The fly may live for a few days, the butterfly for five. An elephant might live for sixty or more years and a whale much longer. But all animal life dies, whether it is consumed for food or fossilized in ageless rock.

It is also true of man: "It is appointed unto men once to die" (Heb. 9:27). We have been forewarned that all of us will die. Every ache and pain is a forerunner of that final collapse of the human system—the grey hair, the uncertain step, the weakening body. Someday our frame will be worn out, we will make out our wills, and our property will be passed on to another. Others will replace us at the workbench, the desk, the home, the pulpit.

Death is a universal experience—for all of us inescapable and inevitable. The thoughts of other creations of God, who have no hereafter, end with death as well. The leaves, the trees, the weeds, the flowers, the lion, the horse, and the faithful dog are gone. And the other types of life, as far as we know, have never asked the question: "After that, what?" Only man asks that.

You and I have a right to get out our "maps" and discover the thrilling journey that lies ahead after death. Paul wrote: "If in this life only we have hope in Christ, we are of all men most miserable" (1 Cor. 15:19).

A dying father once said to his son, "I am leaving this house to you when I go."

The son replied, "Daddy, will you have a house where you are going?"

We have an answer to give to our sons, an answer Jesus gave to us:

> Let not your heart be troubled: ye believe in God, believe also in me. In my Father's house are many mansions: if it were not so, I would have told you. I go to prepare a place for you. And if I go and prepare a place for you, I will come again, and receive you unto myself; that where I am, there ye may be also. And whither I go ye know, and the way ye know (John 14:1-4).

People face death in many ways. Some face it courageously, philosophically, but some with great fear.

THE ANNIHILATIONIST

Some believe that at death all life—physical, mental, and spiritual—becomes extinct, that it no longer exists. They would say "Eat, drink, and be merry, for tomorrow we die." The end of it all is a pile of ashes and a skull.

The Hindu religion teaches that the dead will be lost in some great superconsciousness—lost altogether as to personality and personal existence. The end of all this struggle, this seventy-five or so years of life will end in a place of oblivion to pain, individual consciousness, or external reality called nirvana.

THE ATHEIST—AGNOSTIC
Those to whom the prospect of life after death is a wish or fancy say we cannot prove life after death or even make reasonable assumptions. There is no unassailable evidence by which they say we can prove eternal life.

Tom Paine, the agnostic, said, "Well, I don't believe there is a God and I thank God for it." Deity and its reality will come out.

Robert Ingersoll, the agnostic, was standing at the graveside of his brother and said these pathetic words: "Death is a narrow vale between two eternities. We strive in vain to look beyond the heights. We cry aloud and the only answer is the echo of our wailing cry. From the voiceless dead there comes no response, but in the hour of death hope sees a star and listening love hears the rustling of angels' wings. There was—there is—no greater man than my brother." This instinctive belief and confidence in another life came to the surface in his remarks.

THE SCIENTIFIC MIND
Some scientists can accept the idea of a life beyond the grave. I was thrilled to stand in the office of Wernher

Von Braun, who sent a rocket with 8½ million pounds of thrust to the moon. Von Braun almost lost his faith as a student in Berlin working for a doctorate in science. Under the Hitler regime, he was shriveling spiritually while advancing scientifically and technologically. He defected to the Allies that he might come to America and give his soul a chance. Von Braun said:

> Many people seem to feel that science has somehow made religious ideas untimely and old-fashioned. But I think science has a real surprise for the skeptic. Science, for instance, tells us that nothing in nature, not even the tiniest particle, can disappear without a trace. Nature does not know extinction. All it knows is transformation.
>
> Now if God applies this fundamental principle to the most minute and insignificant parts of His universe, does it not make sense to assume that He also applies it to the human soul? I think it does.
>
> Everything that science has taught me and continues to teach me strengthens my belief in the continuity of our spiritual existence after death. Nothing disappears without a trace and neither will I.

Sir Arthur Compton, the great Nobel Prize winner in geophysics, was thought by some to be the greatest physicist in the world. He said, "Ever since I was a boy, Jesus has been the ideal I would like to live by. . . . I love Him, I honor Him, I worship Him. . . . He has become my Hero-God and I hope that by walking in His footsteps I shall someday inherit eternal life."

Blaise Pascal once said,

> The immortality of the soul is so important, it touches us so deeply, that we cannot remain indifferent to this question unless we have lost all interest in life. According as we have hope or have not hope of all eternal blessings, all our acts and thoughts are directed to such divergent channels that in all common sense we cannot pursue our way without determining its direction.

Pascal knew we had to see life from this high point of view—the eternal perspective. If we simply and finally die like animals why not merely live as animals?

PHILOSOPHY

At their best, philosophers have believed in some form of eternal life. It was said of Socrates: "Is there any wish we can fulfill for you? How shall we bury you?"

"What do you say? You will bury me? You can bury my body but you cannot bury my soul," he replied.

Carved upon a tombstone was this inscription: "Only a body." Cicero in his "Immortality of the Soul," said:

> The question of what comes after death lies close to everyone's heart. Did the great men who lived and died for our country think that at the end of their earthly lives even their names would disappear? Rooted somehow or other in the soul is a premonition . . . and everyone is agreed that there is something that refers to those who have departed this life and we ought to make this same opinion our own.

WORLD RELIGIONS

I once saw some Chinese marching in a funeral procession after burning in effigy paper furniture, horses, food, and the like, trusting that the departed might in reality have these things in the life to come. Muslims have sensed a future existence, though they conceive of it largely as something sensual and material. I saw people in India at their burning ghats cremating the corpses of their dead, trusting that after the fire had consumed the body for two days that person might have two limbs and after four days, four limbs, and after eleven days, even head and mind restored in another life. Others offer their corpses to the birds of the air, hoping that in such devouring the dead might have eternal life. The Hottentots, a former primitive tribe of Africa, had their hopes of eternal life. The Egyptians built their pyramids at great cost, hoping that their carefully embalmed and carefully protected bodies would somehow be preserved for eternal life in the kingdoms to come. The Greeks put coins in the mouths of their dead in hopes it would pay for the trip over death's bridge across the River Styx and bring them eternal life.

A hope for some kind of existence beyond the grave seems alive in the hearts of most all people created originally in God's image.

THE MORALIST

One who feels, from a moral standpoint, that the Creator who put in the human heart this hunger for eternal life believes that God is under obligation to furnish us with some kind of eternal life. In order to fulfill for him and his divine purpose and program, more is expected than this little span of years could produce. Such a plan could only be performed if life had an eternal base. Would it be just for a child to die in infancy without any possibility of completing any purpose in life? What of the student who graduates in June with high hopes and dies in a car wreck in August?

Expecting something beyond—the completion of an inner purpose, would not God bear us into some area of possibility that will allow us to come to some completion of that part in God's eternal plan? Could it be fair of the Creator to have us born with great expectations and then find that the end of life is nothing but a pile of ashes? These are questions the moralist would ask about eternal life.

The great program of God for man demands some duration of life for those who would serve him. These greater instincts of our lives can only be supplied in the greater life that is to follow earthly existence. When God gives us desires, he satisfies them. When he gave the human baby hunger, he supplied it with his mother's breast. When God created the need for a mate, he also created them male and female. When he created the desire to breathe, he created also the air and lungs and respiratory organs for this need. When he gave us aims and purposes unfulfilled in three score and ten years, does it not seem he also intends to give us a chance of fulfilling these great desires which he has put within us?

Moral and spiritual wisdom demands an answer to these questions. We are face to face here with the truth of fractions. Take the number seventy-five, the approximate number of years of our physical lives. Draw a line beneath this number and write below it a million or a billion endless years—remembering that our souls never perish, being eternal spirits that will live forever with God. Then convert that common fraction to a decimal fraction—it will require you to write so many zeros after the decimal point that you will probably have writer's cramp before you set down a single integer. Realize therefore that this life, this span of seventy-five years, is such an infinitesimally small part of the great eternity shaped for our souls.

These pages are penned not for the numerator thinkers, whose only interest is in the now, but for the denominator thinkers, who want to consider life on the basis of at least a billion endless years!

Every good artist wants depth in his picture, that it may be admired and judged as great. You and I who take the brush of life in action and thought and splash the picture of our lives on canvas, must never permit it to be flat, without a horizon, without far-flung skies, without the height of heaven, the great span of spiritual wisdom, lest we put down our brush and leave with the world a work pathetic in its mediocrity. Let these pages be penned for artists with depth and horizons and eternal perspective.

THE CHRISTIAN PHILOSOPHY

Paul wrote: "If in this life only we have hope in Christ, we are of all men most miserable" (1 Cor. 15:19). Elsewhere he wrote: "Eye hath not seen, nor ear heard, neither have entered into the heart of man, the things which God hath prepared for them that love him"

(1 Cor. 2:9). No telescope can focus upon the house "not made with hands"—eternal in the heavens he wrote about (2 Cor. 5:1). One cannot prove it by astronomy, but that does not mean that we don't believe it.

I remember marching in an academic procession side by side with astronaut John Glenn, who was going to receive an honorary degree. We did not have long to talk, so we went immediately to the spiritual effect the stratosphere had upon his life. He said, "It gave me a new idea of the immensity of my Father and my God."

Gagarin, the agnostic Russian cosmonaut, said, "Well, I didn't see any house not made with hands in the heavens up there, nor did I see your God you boast so much about."

Glenn replied, "My God is too big to see, Gagarin!"

It is true that nobody has returned from that realm to tell us what is there except Jesus Christ, who was with the Father in the beginning. Moses and Elijah appeared for awhile, but they gave us no information—they had come to the mountain only to see Christ transfigured in his glory and to display their salute to his excellence. But we learned nothing of the life beyond for them. Only Christ has been there and knows what is there, who is there, and what is to come.

The Bible unfolds to us his divine desire to present to us the incredible riches of the things that God has prepared for those who love him. Without his Word a curtain of darkness would have been pulled down.

Mental syllogisms cannot conjure up our beliefs in eternal life. The Holy Spirit has revealed them to us (1 Cor. 2:10), and we know we have "an house not made with hands, eternal in the heavens" (2 Cor. 5:1).

YOUTH DEMANDS THE LONG, LONG LOOK

The last few years have hurled us into the new space age. Scientists have launched their satellites into orbit. With technical skill and courage they reached the moon, drove vehicles and walked on its surface with the seeming ease of a stroll through a city park. Suddenly freed from the prison of the "here," we make our way into the "out there."

The government published a manual for teaching children entitled, "What's Up There," subtitled, "A Source Book in Space Oriented Mathematics for Grades Five through Eight." It began with the statement: "The space program has given boys and girls throughout the land new heroes and a dramatic frontier with which to identify."

Is that enough? Already we are weary of moon shots and half-heartedly respond to the circling of Mars and Jupiter. "What's up there?" is becoming more important to many than "What's out there among the moon, stars, and planets?" The greatest day in history was not when the astronaut took his first step on the moon. The greatest day in history was two thousand years ago when the Son of God put his foot on the soil of Palestine to give this planet a prospect and promise of what lies in the future.

How pathetic is any educational system for youth that is fascinated with the *out there* without any future of the *out there*. Youth is more and more demanding a look into the future. We are under obligation to inform young people that it is possible for them to know "what God has prepared for those who love him" (1 Cor. 2:9, RSV).

Recently in a high school department of a certain

dynamic church the students demanded a three-month study of the future and what lay in store for mankind. They were tiring of the mere *now* and were demanding a glimpse into the day after tomorrow to know what God had planned. Many youth today are demanding to know whether the end of this life will be more than a pile of ashes and a skull.

Christ put himself under tremendous obligation to both youth and the aged when he said, "I am come that they might have life, and that they might have it more abundantly" (John 10:10). The young ruler came to him asking, "Good Master, what good thing shall I do, that I may have eternal life?" (Matt. 19:16). He evidently had every confidence that Christ knew the answer. When he received the answer, however, he turned away—the conditions seeming too severe.

Today, myriads of young people, still burdened with the young ruler's question, are willing to pay the price that they may have the answer. On hundreds of campuses I have seen students groping among irresponsible cults, spirit movements, unusual philosophies—eastern and western, and other weird speculations. Many of them end up still in the dark, fearful, even suicidal. But Jesus said, "Let not your hearts be troubled. . . . I go to prepare a place for you."

2
DEATH IS UNIVERSAL

NATURE LIVES ON A CONSTANT DIET. Plants wither, die, and become the rich loam and sod in which future plants grow and survive. Animals devour other animals and live on the nourishment within their dead bodies.

The telephone wires are lifted on trees that died. Houses are fashioned from logs that once were alive in the forest. Coal was once dead vegetation, hardened under pressure and years of aging.

Human beings live on the death of nature. A woman eats the oyster that died; a man relishes the turkey that perished for his table, and the turkey in turn fattened on the dead grass and grain in its craw. Snails and slugs feast on the plants they destroy. We concoct medicines that destroy germ life when it threatens our own.

If human life did not die, all processes of birth and propagation would not be necessary along with the privilege of motherhood and fatherhood. When men decided they would be no longer enslaved by captors and enemies, they as patriots, for love of country, bought our freedom with their lives. The armies of scientists, doctors, and nurses have arrayed themselves against the advance of death, yet it remains a stubborn enemy.

The writing of our wills, the purchase of burial plots, the fashioning of the catafalques all salute the inevitability of death. Death, therefore, is of universal interest.

This certainty of death will naturally be followed by the question of Job: "If a man die, shall he live again?" The rich fool of Luke 12 was a "successful" failure because after he had amassed all his wealth he found that night that his soul would be required of him and he had forgotten to ask the question: "... then whose shall these things be, which thou hast provided?" (v. 20).

The great British statesman, William Gladstone, was questioned by a young man regarding his career and his future. "What are your plans for the future?" Gladstone asked him.

The young man said, "Well, sir, I hope to study law."

"Yes, young man, what then?"

"I hope to gain entrance to the bar of England."

"Yes, young man, what then?"

"Then I hope I might find a place in parliament."

"What then?" Gladstone asked again.

"Then I hope, even as you, to do great things for Britain."

"Yes, what then?"

"I suppose I'll die, Mr. Gladstone."

Gladstone replied, "Yes, that is true. What then?"

The young man answered, "Well, I haven't thought any farther than that, sir."

Gladstone said, "Why don't you go home and think life through?" We need to do that too—think life through, to take the long look.

Jesus Christ never took death lightly. He wept at the tomb of Lazarus when death was robbing him for a time of the friendship of one who had become very dear to his heart. Of course, he took away its sting when he raised Lazarus from the dead. Jesus once stepped over to the bier of the son of the widow of Nain and restored him to his mother's arms. He did say to Jairus' daughter, "Arise," and for a time the sting of death was gone, but he did not totally cancel it out. He would not be delivered from death himself, but saw in it the possibility of eventual glorious victory, and for the joy that was set before him endured the cross, and "is set down at the right hand of . . . God" (Heb. 12:2). He saw that even the death of the righteous could lead to a wonderful victory.

No religion or philosophy is adequate that skirts the certainty of death or neglects the desire to understand it and to rob it of its sting.

Why do men die? There are some very interesting theories being propounded. Some say it is because man was disobedient. God said to Adam and Eve, ". . . for in the day that you eat of it [the fruit of the tree of the knowledge of good and evil] you shall die" (Gen. 2:17, RSV).

Professor Jacques Corvoisier once said, "The order of the established Creator was indispensable to life. Man's violation of it leads to death. . . . Death does not figure as the end of a natural process but as the result of things disordered at the beginning. God still permits us, and in his mercy, aids us, to delay the outcome and to prolong this life and struggle."

Dr. Paul Tournier and C. S. Lewis suggested that man, as created, originally was immune from death. He might have been immortal if he had not broken the laws of God.

We note the longevity of the earliest persons as recorded in Genesis 5. If the number of years are to be taken literally, then Adam lived 940 years; Seth 912; Enoch 365; Cainan 910; Methuselah 969. Scholars have attributed the longevity of these people to what is termed symbiosis.

SYMBIOSIS

According to this theory, when God created humanity it was composed of the spirit and the flesh. They were pictured as a horse and its rider. For a time the spirit of man, his God-consciousness and God-control, his higher motivation, his desire to please God and conform to his will were paramount. This was the rider, who controlled the horse, which symbolizes the flesh. The flesh was man's bodily desires, his longings, passions, physical needs, and human aspirations. Add his self-expression, decision-making, and ego in control of his dreams and determinations.

Paul spoke of this dual personality that belonged to him and how the desires of the flesh fight against the spirit—the horse was bucking and getting out of control. The spirit of man, who was trying to control the reins, was losing his power to guide.

This powerful steed of the mundane, lesser flesh was beginning to have its selfish way. The spirit of Cain is pictured as rising up in a fit of jealousy and slaying the Abel of a high moral purpose of obedience to God. Man is beginning to shorten his life span because of the inability of these two facets of humanity getting together in helpful cooperation. One of the philosophers said that if the age figures suggested in Genesis are realistic rather than figurative, then the shorter span of life might have to do with the spirit being unable to control the flesh, causing a partial destruction of this God-willed symbiotic life.

Man is a composite being—meant to be so. He is body and soul. If the body of man dominates the soul, then an imbalance is set up that shortens the life span.

We can hasten death. *Alcohol* knocked some six million men out of industry in one year and actuaries say the habitual drinker can shorten his life by ten years—veritable suicide. *Nicotine* is estimated to have brought about the lung cancer deaths of ninety thousand in a year to say nothing of deaths through heart disease to which it contributed. *Drugs* can kill. The increased use of LSD, marijuana—the pill bottles and the needles—have brought about many new broken chromosomes, insanity, suicides, and early deaths.

Wars continue to debilitate our ranks. A historian said, "We have killed more people in the first fifty years of the twentieth century than died in the previous eight hundred years because of the massive killing power of our arms systems."

A polluted environment can hasten death. Former Senator Harold Hughes has warned us that this continued waste of our natural resources could hasten this earth's becoming a "deadly dung heap."

Twelve thousand youths attempted *suicide* on university campuses in one year alone, simply because life for them no longer held meaning. Our aimlessness is often fatal.

Human carelessness kills thousands annually. We live in a mechanical age and cars become lethal weapons when they carry beneath their hoods hundreds of white horses of power, and when at the wheel careless drivers take over. A quarter-million people were destroyed by carelessness in driving last year, and one-half of them involved drinking or drunken drivers.

Lack of Sabbath rest kills. Man has a built-in seven-day clock both mentally and physically. God said, "Six days you shall labor, and do all your work; but the seventh day is a sabbath [day of rest] . . ." (Exod. 20:9, RSV). In Pittsburgh, a company manufacturing bells for typewriters had great difficulty in getting the metal to give forth a brilliant ring. A metallurgist studying their problem said, "You must cool down the metal. The molecules must rest for one-seventh of the time." Working out this mechanical problem, the bells produced a brilliant ring.

The rest principle is true in the animal kingdom. In the days of the forty-niners, when some wanted to travel seven days a week in order to get to the West speedily, they found their horses gave out sooner than the ones that had rested one day in seven.

The principle is true of humanity. Lord Shaftsbury of the British parliament used to neglect the Sabbath by bringing home his legal books and poring over them during the day, neglecting the laws of God and the higher knowledge and the nourishment of the Word of God. When he lost his sanity one of his colleagues said, "Poor Lord Shaftsbury, he lost his sanity because of his neglect of the Sabbath." Is this farfetched?

A well-known surgeon once reminded us that "If Christ was Co-creator with the Father and that 'without him was nothing made that was made,' then his Christian laws must be healthy laws."

Some of our spiritual neglect has to do with our physical welfare. Body and soul can catch each other's diseases.

There are some, on the other hand, who die early from good causes. There have been the martyrs of the arena, some of them young people, who went singing to their deaths for the service of Christ. We have thousands who have been wiped out in concentration camps, not for lack of faith but because of it. Many are facing starvation today, and many have come to know death because of various holocausts even in contemporary history. I have known several missionaries who died early because of their faithfulness. Willing to work in areas without a balanced diet, they fall prey to malnutrition and disease. Some have been overworked in their faithfulness. One widowed mother with eight children had worked and toiled tirelessly. When she died a few of her children got together and put this on her tombstone: "This woman died of too much loving, scrubbing, nursing, washing." Her death was premature because of her consecration, her conscience, and her concern.

Christ died in his early thirties, but for a cause that was based upon our good. In his sacrifice, we often find courage for our long, long look.

There are two kinds of death. Man is a soul. He only has a body. This is the fundamental principle we must always keep in mind. The Bible does not make very much of physical death. The purpose of a watch is to tell time; therefore, the works of the watch are the most important part. It is possible for an accident to destroy the watch case and yet the watch will go on ticking, telling its proper time. It is possible to crush the human body and yet the soul of man will go on having kinship with God. When we have destroyed the body we have not actually destroyed the personality.

We make so much of the separation of the soul from the body, as though this were the one tragic separation of life. True, it can bring sorrow and loneliness. But for a Christian to depart and be with Christ, Paul says, "is far better" (Phil. 1:23). Paul claimed that, while he was a prisoner of his body (this tenement of clay) "[he was] absent from the Lord." But when our souls shall leave these bodies, we shall be "present with the Lord" (2 Cor. 5:6, 8). It is rather shocking to behold the terror that strikes some people, even Christians, at the time of departure of a loved one.

If to depart is to be with Christ, then the only problem that remains for Christians at the time of death of a loved one is in adjusting to one's own separation, and there are pangs here even though we have faith in the hereafter. Jesus wept at the tomb of Lazarus, but they were not tears of despair.

God has outlined for us our average expectancy of life. However, now, with the help of medicine and other discoveries which have been at the encouragement of our Creator, we have seen the lengthening of life, especially among those in their seventies.

But, "It is appointed unto man once to die," and this is our expectation and this is part of God's plan. Death is that time when all respiration has stopped, the heart has ceased to function, and the soul has laid down this tabernacle of clay. Paul said, "For in this [house, that is, in this tent] we groan, earnestly desiring to be clothed upon with our house which is from heaven" (2 Cor. 5:2).

CHRIST'S ANSWER TO DEATH

The death of an infant is a kind of loss very difficult to accept. When God says, "Suffer little children to come unto me," how could he do this to a child who has not had a chance to even live and know the purpose for which he was born, much less to complete it and carry it out? There is no answer to this; we just have to trust our little ones to the Everlasting Arms, which are sufficient. One mother beautifully voiced this trust in her poem written as she looked across to the bedroom window of her neighbor's house:

> *Mother, I see you in your nursery light*
> *Leading your babies all in white*
> *To their sweet rest.*

Christ, the Good Shepherd, carries mine tonight,
And that is best.

You tremble each hour because your arms
Your heart is wrung with alarms
And sore oppressed;
My darlings are safe—out of reach of harm
And that is best.

But grief is selfish and I cannot see
Always why I should so stricken be
More than the rest;
But I know that, as well as for them, for me,
God did the best.

The time of our physical death being unknown to us means we should be ready to undergo the experience at any time without fear or unpreparedness. One of the difficulties that people have with the timing of death is death in infancy.

When I was in Pittsburgh I had the wedding of a handsome young couple. They were happy as they knelt at the altar, full of joyous expectation. Four days later I conducted the funeral of the bride. They were on their honeymoon and, driving late at night, they accidentally drove into the rear of a truck with no taillights and the young bride was killed instantly.

We do not know. A young man dies at the early age of thirty—his life vested with thorough educational preparation, dominant of purpose and fortified with many outstanding talents that promised many years of outstanding service. Someone exclaimed almost in anger, "What a tragedy! God shouldn't allow his service to be cut off at so early an age!"

Strange how some people think. "The service cut off?" Be careful, Christians, what you say. Have we not read that there in the other country, "They serve him day and night in his temple?" Whatever we are doing in the heavenly places we are busy at our God-given tasks, with which we have fallen in love, without any fatigue, without any discouragement, without worry, or weariness, or fear of defeat, or failure. What will we be doing in heaven? It certainly is not the end of our vital service. There will be serving with a fervor and a joy unknown on earth.

This is why youth need the thrill of a long, long look. I was giving a week of addresses at Dartmouth College and the president was driving me around the campus. We paused at the front of one of the fraternity houses. He said, "A tragedy happened here some time ago. Nine fraternity men died in their beds from asphyxiation—from gas escaping into their rooms while they slept. We shall never forget that tragic night when nine caskets were lined up in Dartmouth chapel. At the funeral service, I said that at a time like this Dartmouth is sheared of its specious sophistries and its petty poses and we look at life in this long, long length and agree with Audrey L. Moore, the essayist, who said, "Man to be truly man must be both rational and religious, and if he is not both then he is neither."

Many collegians today are looking down the long line with a glance at eternity, realizing the insufficiency of life without prospect.

Robert Ingersoll, the agnostic, was lying in his casket, immaculately clothed in death as he always was in life. A friend paused for a moment, and stood looking into the face of his departed friend. Remembering

Ingersolls's lack of spiritual confidence, he said, "Poor, Bob—all dressed up and no place to go!"

Some communists might scoff, accusing Christians of living in "the sweet by-and-by." But what do men do without a by-and-by? It is a part of the classic nature of our faith. "If in this life only we have hope in Christ, we are of all men most miserable" (1 Cor. 15:19).

Human beings are said to be tetrads (four-part beings): body, mind, soul, and spirit. If we define *soul* as being emotions, then souls are not only in man but in the animals as well, for they demonstrate fear, hate, anger, and courage. We may be as sly as a fox, as tender as a kitten, as mad as a hornet, as gruff as a bear, or as faithful as a dog. All these expressions deal with emotional life. But man's soul is more than emotion. Man is a soul, inbreathed with the Spirit of God, which gives him more than the animals and what animals do not have. Unlike in the animals, the spirit within becomes man's guide. The soul is, in a sense, our violin, but the tune that is played, whether it be discordant or harmonious, is dependent upon the spirit of man which is the violinist. This new life was offered Israel in the renewal by the Spirit of God within the soul of man. Ezekiel wrote: "I will put a new spirit within you; and I will take the stony heart out of their flesh . . . and will give them an heart of flesh: that they may walk in my statutes, and keep mine ordinances" (Ezek. 11:19, 20).

When the Spirit of God is inbreathed to us, then it is the Spirit that determines the action and attitude of the soul. The soul then becomes the instrument upon which the Spirit plays until the Spirit dominates the songs we sing, the words we speak, the thoughts we think—the whole tenor of our lives. This is the guidance that makes man human, that gives him a spirit as well as a soul.

When death comes, the human instrument may fall into decay, but the spirit of man functions without these physical instruments.

There is a second death. This is not the separation of the soul from the body. This second death is the separation of the spirit of man from God because unforgiven sin comes in between. If the soul is separated from God because unforgiven sin comes in between, then the great problem of all moral philosophers is: "How do we get rid of this sin that separates man from God, bringing about this second death?"

We shall not make light of the Greek philosophers, who did their best to discover who God was and to come to a solution for this problem of sin. Socrates had cried out to his pupil, "Plato, I know God will forgive sin but I canot see how." The Greek religion came up with no satisfactory solution as to how sin might be removed between man and God to conquer this spiritual death.

Paul, with all the subtleties of his Socratic mind, could find no other solution for sin but the fact that God sent his only begotten Son to be the propitiation for our sins (Rom. 3:25). In that gift, in which God gave all he had, his Son, and the Son gave all he had, his life, we have the solution for the sin problem. So now, "if we confess our sins, he is faithful and just to forgive us our sins, and to cleanse us from all unrighteousness" (1 John 1:9).

God has said that he places our sins behind his back (Isa. 38:17). It means he has placed our sins so that there is nothing now between us and him, and gives us an "at-one-ment" with God because sin is removed. This is his gracious system of salvation.

Christ said, "He that believeth in me, though he were dead [soul separated from body], yet shall he live [not separated from God but alive eternally in his presence]" (John 11:25).

Often when a bee stings, it leaves its stinger in the wound and goes away to die—powerless to sting again. Death stung Christ on the cross, left its sting in him, and is now defeated, and powerless to harm a believer. "The sting of death is sin. . . . But thanks be to God, which giveth us the victory through our Lord Jesus Christ" (1 Cor. 15:56, 57).

When death visits our homes, Christians, let us be careful how we react, for the world is watching us.

VICTORIOUS DEATH OF CHRISTIANS

Paul had a joyous view of death, seeing it as a victorious departure from this world. Even as a ship tied to the dock and moored to the wharf of this world by this thin line that we call life is ready to take its departure across the well-charted waters, so we are headed for heaven, our final homeland.

Paul said to the Christians, "The time of my departure is at hand." To the Christian, life in its larger sense is not a little lake bounded by mundane hills. It is a large sea stretched before us. We must not be so bound up in this world that we lose the sight of the glory on the other side.

When I was eleven, I remember when my sister Dorothy died of spinal meningitis at the age of fourteen. Here was a beautiful uncompleted life. The man who conducted her funeral said, "Dorothy was one of the finest Christian girls I had ever known."

I used to stand at the door of her room. It became rather a shrine for me because it was there I had my first experience with death. I, a frightened boy, had stood there and seen my father holding Dorothy's hand. He motioned me to his side. He said, "Dodo, do you know who is holding your hand?"

She replied, "Yes, Jesus is holding my hand." Those were her last words.

To a great degree, these words took out of my boyish heart the sting of death, taking hold of the hand of Jesus Christ. As I write, this experience among my own loved ones and others is dear to my heart.

After Dorothy's death, I asked my father, "Dad, didn't it shake your faith and make you wonder why God's will should bring this to pass and wipe out Dorothy's future and your dreams for her?"

He said, "Son, remember when you would ask me for things and the answer was no? You were too young to understand why I had to deny you those things then, but you will understand in later years. When you ask now, you just trust that Dad loves you, in the absence of an explanation. Now God, as my heavenly Father is, asking this of me, his son, to trust him in the absence of an explanation. I am willing to do for God, my Father, what you did for me—trust."

Susan, a mother of several children had fought cancer and death. One of her friends wrote: "At her funeral the group of mourners was small. Perhaps others had felt as I, that they lacked the strength to stand at her graveside in the bright summer sunshine. We had known for a long time that Susan was living with cancer. There had been surgery, radium treatments, drug experiments. Her body was ravaged, but somehow one was never aware of this. There was a shining light about her. How trite to say that she wore a halo, but she did. She wept and even cursed the pain and inconvenience, but she lived every day God gave her with love. Somehow I expected God to grant Susan a miracle. I knew the prognosis, yet I was unprepared for this moment at the grave.

"The service was brief. I watched her children, calm and dry-eyed as each took a rose from the spray on the casket—Susan had prepared them well for this hour of sorrow. Her sister, as shaken as I, said, 'Perhaps Susan was granted her miracle to do what she must. She prepared her children for this moment and now she is free of pain—her spirit is soaring.' "

Have we prepared our children if death should touch our homes and dear ones? Many parents and teachers explain to youth the facts and wonders of birth—our entrance into this life. Why not share with them the possible glory and meaning of our exit from the life that so engages our interests here? Remember how many of the graves today are of young people.

When D. L. Moody was dying, they revived him with a stimulant and sustained him for a short time, but he said, "Let me go. I see Dwight, Irene. Heaven is opening and earth is receding. This is my coronation day!" Moody slipped happily into eternal life.

John Huss, that great Christian martyr, lifted his face as he was being burned at the stake and said, "Oh God, for another life to give for Jesus' sake."

Stephen, as the stones were hurled in hatred outside Jerusalem's city gates, lay dying and said, "I see Jesus sitting at the right hand of God—Father, lay not this sin to their charge." Gloriously, Stephen entered into the presence of his God.

Peter, it is said, received the promise of Christ as to how he would die: by crucifixion. Yet, as they fastened him to the cross was said to say, "I am not worthy to die as my Master, head upward. Tie me head downward, please." This they did, and later they could see his calloused feet which had trod many roads with the tireless message received from the Lord, held high in the air. They saw the blood trickling from his back where they had scourged him to beat down the possible strength that might be remaining. Thus he died victoriously. Caesar was told that another enemy of Rome had died, but it was Peter who lived and Rome that was dying.

Paul was warned against going to Rome for the fear that they might seize him. Paul went fearlessly to meet the sentence of death against those who refused to worship Caesar. He said, "The time of my departure is at hand. I have fought a good fight, I have kept the faith, I have finished my course. There is therefore laid up for me a crown of righteousness." It was said that he was marched past the Three Fountains, where the burned corpses of believers were still hanging at the place of execution. There he was accorded the honorable death by beheading, because he was a Roman citizen, and they would not subject him to the shame of dying on a cross.

Rome rejoiced about its imagined victory over these two giants of the Kingdom. But Rome was dying and Caesar doomed to extinction. But beneath the city of Rome, down in the catacombs, among the tombs were Christians worshiping, singing the songs of the Father and the Lamb. While Rome was burning, the Kingdom of God was marching on to its final victory over death.

3
THE INTERMEDIATE STATE

BY THE INTERMEDIATE STATE, WE REFER to the place and condition of our departed loved ones between the time of their death and the resurrection that is to come. It is only natural that because of the love that God has placed in us, we are curious about those departed loved ones. Our hearts and minds are filled with such questions as, "God, where are they?" We ask, "Are they safe? Are they happy? Are they in your presence? Are they aware of us? Is all well with them?"

We have some blanket assurances. One of them is found in Psalm 16: "In thy presence is fulness of joy; at thy right hand there are pleasures for evermore."

Do our questions irk God when our demands for knowing are so insistent? Is the information we obtain concerning the present condition of our departed loved ones a prize to be gained only after having paid a great price for our inordinate curiosity? The Apostle Paul told of an experience of being caught up to the third heaven. He said concerning this experience:

> And to keep me from being too elated by the abundance of revelations, a thorn was given me in the flesh, a messenger of Satan, to harass me, to keep me from being too elated. Three times I besought the Lord about this, that it should leave me; but he said to me, "My grace is sufficient for you, for my power is made perfect in weakness." I will all the more gladly boast of my weaknesses, that the power of Christ may rest upon me. For the sake of Christ,

then, I am content with weaknesses, insults, hardships, persecutions, and calamities; for when I am weak, then I am strong (2 Cor. 12:7-10, RSV).

What was the physical "thorn in the flesh" that Paul had to bear? It might have been an eye disease, for the Galatians said in a letter to him that they would gladly have plucked out their eyes and given them to Paul—as if he needed a new pair. Whatever the infirmity of the flesh was, it was in order to keep him from being proud because of the unusual information. Was it knowledge concerning the departed that he had insisted upon knowing?

Some years ago a very devoted minister underwent a similar experience. The Rev. William Tennant had a vision during a time when he was in uncertain health and fainted one day. The trance stayed with him, and at the time, friends in alarm called in a doctor, who declared him to be dead. They prepared him for burial and his friends assembled for the funeral. Suddenly his eyes opened and he came back to health, except that his mind was blank. His memory returned to him slowly. Reluctantly he told of his experience during the trance: "I was in another sphere, guided by heavenly beings. The music was ravishingly melodious and glorious. Innumerable hosts of happy beings were there. I had not long stayed, for I must return to earth. In doing so I was shocked out of all active life and only slowly did I recover from the revelation, which had been too much for me." Many accepted this story by Tennant because he was a man of such exceptional credibility and reputation.

The question arises: "May we be guilty of the kind of curiosity that is too costly for us? Should we leave more to God in faith, trusting him about the future?"

ENCOURAGEMENTS TO INQUIRE

We cannot discover where our loved ones are by telescope or celestial camera. Not enough information has come to us from those from the "other side" to know. Nor by mental gymnastics can we know what is there or what our loved ones are doing. Should we draw down the curtain and say we must go on in the darkness of ignorance? No. Paul wrote "God has revealed to us through the Spirit . . . even the depths of God" (1 Cor. 2:10, 11, RSV). God has revealed to us everything we need to know about our loved ones after death.

VIEWS HELD ABOUT THE FUTURE OF THE DEPARTED

According to the view of annihilation, which we looked at earlier, death brings destruction to both body and soul. Man dies—that is the end. As the flower of the field he flourishes and then is gone and the world knows him no more. We perish as the flower.

But we believe that the soul is an eternal thing—it is imperishable. It lives forever with God. It lives without God if one decides to choose the other way, but the soul is everlasting and eternal even though the body perishes.

According to some people, the soul, at the time of death, falls into unconsciousness and is not awakened until the resurrection, a state called *soul sleep*. Various Scriptures have been used in reference to death as sleep. Matthew recorded concerning the resurrection of Christ: "And many bodies of the saints who had fallen asleep were raised" (Matt. 27:52, RSV). "Our friend Lazarus has fallen asleep" (John 11:11, RSV). Paul wrote: "God will bring with him those who have fallen asleep" (1 Thess. 4:14, RSV). Concerning Jairus' daughter Jesus said, "She is not dead but sleeping" (Luke 8:52, RSV). Although he said Lazarus was sleeping, he said plainly later on that Lazarus was dead.

The word *sleep* may simply be used symbolically or euphemistically as a tender term in consideration of feelings. It refers to the body, stilled into inactivity as a slumbering individual. Bodily, those who are asleep neither converse nor praise or take note of personal bodily things. And since we don't accept death as final, it is obvious why the figurative language is used.

ABSENT FROM THE BODY— PRESENT WITH THE LORD

A number of Scriptures deal with the state of the departed dead. One of the most significant is the Apostle Paul's statement: "We know that while we are at home in the body we are away [absent] from the Lord. . . . We would rather be away from the body and at home [present] with the Lord" (2 Cor. 5:6, 8, RSV).

Some say Paul was talking about the second coming of Christ when we will be with God—when we will have our new resurrection bodies. Others say Paul meant that at death, when we desert this body, we—our souls—go immediately to be with Christ. We do not have to wait for our resurrection bodies to be with him.

Paul wrote "But we would not have you ignorant, brethren, concerning those who are asleep, that you may not grieve as others do who have no hope. For since we believe that Jesus died and rose again, even so, through Jesus, God will bring with him those who have fallen asleep [whose bodies are dead but whose souls are alive with him]" (1 Thess. 4:13, 14, RSV).

When Christ comes at the first resurrection, he will bring these with him. The word in Greek means "bring along with him." He could not bring them along with him if they had not been with him.

Jude prophesied "Behold, the Lord came with his holy myriads, to execute judgment on all" (Jude 14, RSV). Here again, if the saints were not with him, he could not bring them along with him.

THE THIEF ON THE CROSS AND PARADISE
When Christ was crucified on Golgotha, he died between two thieves—two men whom he desired in his last hour to save. The thief on the left cursed him between gasping throes of agony. The thief on the right, however, was penitent and said that he himself was getting his just deserts but that Jesus had done nothing amiss.

The question presented is "Where did the thief go immediately after his death?" Note both his request and his dying confession, as recorded by Luke: "And he said unto Jesus, Lord, remember me when thou comest into thy kingdom. And Jesus said unto him, 'Verily I say unto thee, To day shalt thou be with me in paradise'" (Luke 23:42, 43).

Theory 1. The translators have put the comma in the wrong place, according to some interpreters of this passage. They say it should come after "today," which is in common usage in the Old Testament as a warning that something very important is about to be said. This introductory expression is used in at least two places in the Old Testament as though he were saying "Verily, verily, I say unto you this day—right now," to prepare the listener for a very important statement about to be made. We read: "And these words which I command you this day shall be upon your heart" (Deut. 6:6, RSV), emphasizing a solemn statement to come. Again, "The statutes, and the ordinances, which I command you this day" (Deut. 7:11, RSV).

Some claim these first words of Jesus were to emphasize the following words after the comma, "Thou shalt be with me in paradise," and that paradise represents a later period on earth when Christ reigns gloriously and in full control.

This "paradise," according to this theory, will not exist until Christ has established a "paradise" on earth, sometime in the future.

Theory 2. Christ was referring to "paradise" that was already established for some of the dead, and that the thief was to go there with Christ immediately, according to this theory.

Before the resurrection of Christ from the dead, many believed that there was a place of the dead where both good and evil went. The place was referred to as hell or Hades. It was thought to have two parts—at the top were the righteous dead, those who had the right attitude toward the Messiah, who had not yet come in the flesh, those who were receptive to the message of Jehovah God. This was called "paradise" or "Abraham's bosom." Below paradise, separated from the top part, was the place called Sheol, or the abiding place of those who loved evil. This place holds the spirits of those who rejected righteousness. After Christ descended into

Theory 2

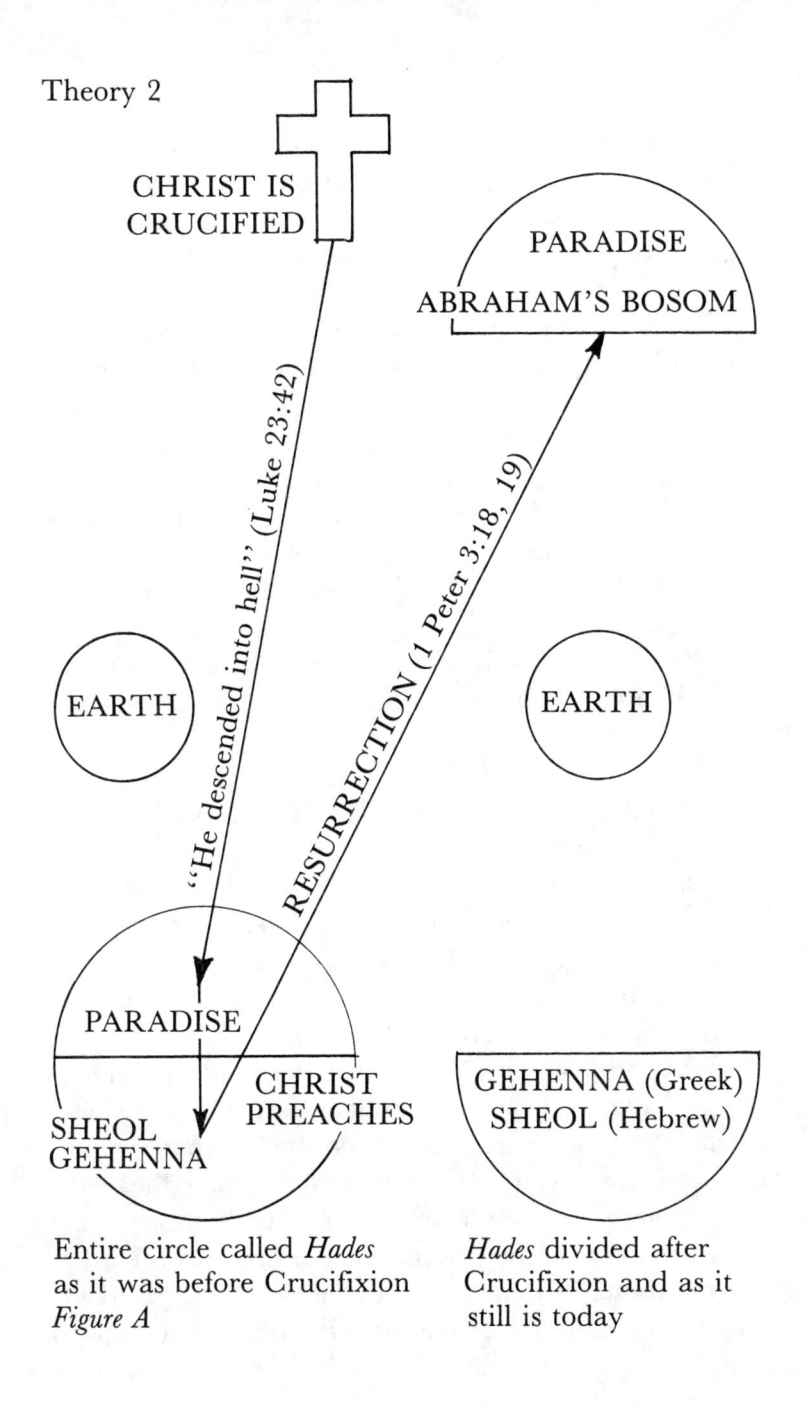

CHRIST IS CRUCIFIED

PARADISE
ABRAHAM'S BOSOM

"He descended into hell" (Luke 23:42)

RESURRECTION (1 Peter 3:18, 19)

EARTH

EARTH

PARADISE

SHEOL
GEHENNA

CHRIST PREACHES

GEHENNA (Greek)
SHEOL (Hebrew)

Entire circle called *Hades* as it was before Crucifixion
Figure A

Hades divided after Crucifixion and as it still is today

hell, all would have had a chance to accept him. These then, with the others in paradise, captives for a time, follow the new Master of their choice up to the new paradise which is now in the presence of God, the abode of the righteous.

What Jesus promised the thief on the cross that day, was not just a paradise that was later to be established on earth in his victorious day. It was the paradise to which Christ first descended and from which he led "captives" up to be with him at the right hand of God. It is this paradise to which Paul referred when he said, "I was caught up into paradise." When Jesus comes he will not come alone. "Behold, the Lord [shall come] with his holy myriads . . . to execute judgment (Jude 14, 15, RSV), also translated, "Behold, the Lord cometh with ten thousands of his saints."

THE RICH MAN AND LAZARUS (Luke 16:19-32)

Theory 1. Some believe that Jesus did not mean that this teaching should be taken literally and that it did not mean to teach that immediately after death the deceased were alive and conscious. An ancient Greek manuscript of this passage contains, at the beginning of this passage, the words "He said, also, another parable," and that "this is not a true story but a parable." Some say that this story is only an extended simile and that it was addressed to the Pharisees who were interested mainly in money and things that they possessed and therefore must not be taken literally.

Abraham and the rich man, according to this theory, were not literally alive or conscious in Hades. Christ is said to be merely teaching here the lesson that what is exalted among men is an abomination in the sight of

God. Other manuscripts do not contain the words identifying this passage as a parable, so most scholars do not accept that interpretation.

Theory 2. Others believe that this story means what it says, reasoning that Christ would not propose things that were not true. They don't believe he would give such wrong impressions. Christ, in the record of the rich man and Lazarus, said that when they departed they went to a very definite place. "The poor man died and was carried by the angels to Abraham's bosom" (v. 22, RSV). That meant that his soul went to the dwelling place of the righteous dead. The rich man died and was buried and went to "Hades" (v. 23). That meant to another part of the place of the dead—the abode of the unrighteous. In the second place they were all conscious and conversed: "He called out . . ." and "Abraham said . . ." (vv. 24, 25).

Memory was active for the departed dead. Abraham said, "Son, remember that in your lifetime. . . ." The rich man was concerned about his brothers. "I have five brothers and I want to send someone to warn them."

Do those who take the view that this story was a parable really believe that Abraham and the rich man were not literally alive? Do they think that they and all others are literally dead until the resurrection? Do they believe that these things never happened as reported? Was this a parable just used to make a striking impact on the critical Pharisees?

Christ's purpose in all he said was not to confuse or to misrepresent. Was it fair to draw a picture of these characters in an after-death location, to picture Abraham as being conscious if he was still unconscious? Why use situations that cannot be so, in order to prove a point that is true? Why raise hope in the listeners that men are alive and conscious after death if these figures are false?

If this story in Luke is only a parable, then why do the scholars not include, "He spake in a parable"? In other translations the authenticity of "in a parable" phrase is made very doubtful by the preponderance of the opposite opinion. Usually Christ when using a parable said "is like unto. . . ." But he did not say that in this case, giving us further indication that this must have been a true story.

COMMUNICATION WITH THE DEPARTED

Some believe we can talk to the dead, since they are conscious. In support of this they call our attention to Saul and his experience with Samuel and the witch of Endor (1 Sam. 28:3-25).

Salient facts can be garnered from these verses. First, Samuel had been Saul's guide, had helped crown him king and had been his closest adviser. Saul, however, consulted Samuel less and less because of his disobedience, and later we read: "And Samuel came no more to see Saul until the day of his death" (1 Sam. 15:35). Saul had stopped talking to God because of his sins of rebellion. But the Spirit of the Lord departed from Saul and an evil spirit of the lord of this world (Satan) troubled him.

Saul, having lost his connection with God through disobedience, was influenced by Satan, who put ideas into Saul's mind because he knew he could influence him through the "familiar spirits." Thus Satan not only caused the death of Saul, and his sons and the destruction of the army of Israel, but also brought misfortune to the entire nation through this episode.

Saul disguised himself with other raiment and went to the witch of Endor. God had, through the prophets and on many other occasions, given very definite commands against the practice of witchcraft or necromancy.

Saul asked his servant to find this woman who had the power of witchcraft and possibly of calling up the dead. Saul was in a bad way. The Philistines had drawn up their forces and were aligned against him, and Saul was afraid. As the Philistines camped their armies in Gilboa, and "when Saul saw the host of the Philistines, he was afraid, and his heart greatly trembled" (1 Sam. 28:5).

Some say that this appearance of Samuel was not merely an imitation of the dead prophet—that the Lord actually permitted Samuel himself to return because of the important message he had to pass on to the errant King Saul. "Then said Samuel, Wherefore then dost thou ask of me, seeing the Lord is departed from thee, and is become thine enemy? And the Lord hath done to him, as he spake by me: for the Lord hath rent his kingdom out of thine hand, and given it to thy neighbour, even to David. . . . The Lord also shall deliver the host of Israel into the hand of the Philistines" (1 Sam. 28:16, 17, 19).

The fact that the witch herself became frightened is other evidence that this occasion, rather than being something we might expect to be repeated on demand, was a special work of God on Saul's behalf.

SPIRITUALISM AS A CULT— NECROMANCY AS A PRACTICE

Necromancy has been forbidden by God: "There shall not be found among you . . . any one who practices divination, a soothsayer . . . or a sorcerer . . . or a medium, or a wizard, or a necromancer. For whoever does these things is an abomination to the Lord. . . . For these nations which you are about to dispossess, give heed to soothsayers and to diviners; but as for you, the Lord your God has not allowed you to do so" (Deut. 18:10-14, RSV).

Paul described to Timothy, pastor at Ephesus, God's attitude toward this practice which was common in that city: "Now the Spirit expressly says that in later times some will depart from the faith [heed false doctrines] by giving heed to deceitful spirits [fooled by trickery] and doctrines of demons" (1 Tim. 4:1, RSV).

So many gullible people have been deceived by trickery. Houdini, the magician, challenged the mediums by offering to pay ten thousand dollars for every trick he could not explain or do himself. The challenge was never taken up. The tricks of sleight of hand, table-rapping, and levitation have taken in many people. Pretended conversations with the departed are numerous.

Sir Oliver Lodge, attending a séance, was told by the leader that he was talking to his son. Asking his son what they were doing in heaven, the son is said to have replied, "Well, up here, Dad, they don't do nothing."

Lodge said to the medium, "My son had a doctorate in English literature. I am confident he would never have used the double negative," and he stalked out in utter indignation.

Another inquired of the medium, "Ask my son what they think about Jesus in heaven." His son allegedly replied, "Why, they don't even mention him up here, and never as Savior."

Paul added to the characteristics and doctrines of demons—the tragic attacks that ensue against Christian convictions in the human mind. "Through the pretense of liars . . ." Paul added, they so often misrepresent the facts. Some mediums may be sincere but they themselves may be under the power of a deceiving spirit.

If God were to permit us to meet our departed loved ones, converse with them, why should it be in some spooky dark room or in some cave in Endor? If this is possible, why not encourage it to be held in God's house, at a prayer meeting? If our friends can talk to us in a place dear and sacred to us, his altars, on our own bended knees, why would this privilege not have come to us through interpreters and human mediators of the spiritual life? If this is a privilege of the Christian, why did not Christ encourage his disciples to practice it and to encourage the flock to do the same? If necromancy, calling back of the dead, is for the Christian, why did not John, Peter, Paul, and Christ encourage us to do the same instead of condemning our attempts to do so? Why do leaders of this cult so often deny the accepted Christian doctrines?

Dr. J. Stafford found that every medium he visited, when asked about his faith, denied the unique deity of Christ, his virgin birth and atoning death. He said when they were questioned about Christ they closed the séance.

THE TRANSFIGURATION (Matt. 17:1-8)
The privileged disciples invited to the great transfiguration on the mountain would never forget the uplifting experience. First of all, it was Jesus who was transfigured before them. They actually saw him.

Moses and Elijah appeared to them—were seen by them. Here the word for "seen" was a passive verb of *orao, ophthein,* which in Greek meant "to appear to." Rather than saying the disciples "saw" them, Matthew said, "they appeared" to them. The two talked to Jesus but had no conversation with the disciples. These two patriarchs talked to Jesus alone. They were there to see Christ transfigured in his glory and after rising to their feet, the disciples saw Jesus only. There is nothing in this passage to encourage us to call back or have speech with any of the great personages of yesterday. When they returned from the mountain, Jesus said to them in warning, "Tell no man of this vision."

Whether or not God permits information to come to us from the dead on their initiative is another question, but the biblical writers state that we are not to trouble the dead on our initiative, which is necromancy.

A father died in 1921 and the only will found, written in 1905, left all the property to his first son. The first son died and the second son had several visions of his father saying, "Son, you will find a newer will in my overcoat pocket." The son found sewn in the inner pocket a paper saying, "Read the twenty-seventh chapter of Genesis in my dad's old Bible." Following these instructions, he found in the Bible another will made in 1919 equally dividing the property among all four sons. This was not done through the use of a medium.

THE CLOUD OF WITNESSES (Heb. 12:1)
"Therefore, since we are surrounded by so great a cloud of witnesses, let us also lay aside every weight, and sin which clings so closely, and let us run with perseverance the race that is set before us, looking to Jesus the pioneer and perfecter of our faith" (Heb. 12:1, 2, RSV).

There are two interpretations of these verses. One is

that our dead, in the presence of Christ, are actually watching us and cheering us on. It is as though they were in the balcony watching us in our efforts in this great game of life, noting our failures and sorrowing over them, noticing our victories and rejoicing. The others ask the question: "Do we really desire that they know of all that is befalling us?" The Bible says that in heaven God will wipe away all tears from our eyes and there shall be no more sorrow nor pain. Do we want our departed ones to grieve over the sins that conquer us? Those hurdles which we knocked down in this clumsy race of life, those times when we were ignobly defeated, those sorrows that plagued us at the separation of loved ones—do we want them to see all that?

JOY IN HEAVEN (Luke 15:7)
Do those with Christ know about the conversion of those on earth and rejoice over it? Do they know of the denials as we face our obligations toward God and his kingdom on earth? "I tell you, there is joy before the angels of God over one sinner who repents" (Luke 15:10, RSV). Notice the "before the angels." The angels are the go-betweens informing God what is happening on this earthly footstool. Because the angels know does not mean that our loved ones should also know.

Many feel that this is the better analysis of the "cloud of witnesses" mentioned in Hebrews 12. It is not their present knowledge of what we are doing that is important but our memory of what they did during their lifetime. It is our memory of what they were that should spur us on.

I often go back to the memory of what my mother was like, all the tenderness and patient long-suffering, and her passion to win others to Christ. I go back to the memory of my father and my introduction to Jesus Christ. The volumes he wrote concerning his faith—the dynamic messages that came from his lips at lectern and pulpit. I want to remember my parents' courage in the face of family bereavement. Their influence is upon us still. Some remind us they are worshiping God day and night in his temple.

As Christ is making intercession for us, in worshiping with Christ it is probable that our loved ones too are joining him in turning their prayers of intercession toward us and our welfare, thus having a place for us still in their conscious memory. As they sing the songs of Zion, it is possible that we may sense the wafting of some of their melodies toward us.

The fishermen of the Adriatic, when they used to make their way out to sea, knew that their wives would gather on the shore and sing a hymn that was often borne to them on a kind breeze blowing in their direction. At times the sailors out on the distant sea, if the winds were kind, would sing a hymn and their voices were borne back to those on the shoreline listening for a song from the men whom they loved.

When we seek for solace and comfort for today and covet confidence and faith for tomorrow, it is enough for us to know we have the guidance of our heavenly Father. Why must people run to astrology and not be sufficiently guided by the Father who put the planets in their courses and who can lead us in our plans for today and tomorrow?

Some so-called Christians would not think of going to work and their tasks for the day without reading their horoscopes in the paper to find out what the writers have to say about Pisces or Aquarius and what is likely to happen to them. But they would not take five minutes to begin the day with the reading of the teachings of Jesus Christ, the Creator of the universe. It is as though they trust more in impersonal signs than they do in the plan of the Son of God.

PURGATORY

Purgatory is said to be a place of purging and punishment after death. It is supposed to be only temporary for the believer. It is considered a "gate" through which we must pass to obtain a glorious complete eternal life.

Many outstanding Christian scholars, especially Roman Catholic, believe in this experience after death. It is based upon the conviction that only the holy can enter heaven—those who are undefiled.

Other religions in part embrace the concept of the necessity of fire after death to guarantee eternal life. I have, in India, seen devotees at their funeral ceremonies, trusting that the offering of human bodies to flame will offer them the propitiation they need to gain entrance into heaven. Certain Greek religions mentioned the "fire regions" where souls were purified and thus freed from their sins and shortcomings.

There have been people in church history who have felt that some take sin altogether too lightly and that there must be definite times and places of their purifying—that God's justice and mercy are harmonized by purgatory. They feel that this purging experience of suffering is pain, but pain with a hope. While it is in a way like the punishment of hell, this place is not an eternal dwelling for the believer. Those who accept this view feel they cannot be completely happy in God until they have suffered. They are willing to suffer a present loss of God in this period, but are fed by the confidence that they are still in his family during the process.

There are others who cannot accept this doctrine of purgatory. They feel that the verse upon which this doctrine has been built has been taken out of context. Paul wrote: "Each man's work will become manifest . . . because it will be revealed with fire, and the fire will test what sort of work each one has done. . . . If any man's work is burned up, he will suffer loss, though he himself will be saved, but only as through fire" (1 Cor. 3:13, 15, RSV).

Paul was not speaking so much of man's redemption as he was about building the Church of Jesus Christ. He had been saying that "other foundation can no man lay than that is laid," which is the man Christ Jesus—and Christ is the great foundation of the Church. If any build a church on any other foundation than this, the fires of time, devastation, and persecution, will see it consumed, as that foundation will simply not meet the test. It is a warning, not about building our salvation upon the wrong foundation and the wrong security but building a perishable church, built upon something other than the divinity of Jesus Christ and on his work.

Our hope is built in Christ—not upon our own suffering. We feel it is possible to insult the efficacy of the cross—as if Christ did not suffer enough so we must make up the lack of his sufficiency of pain. It is said that if any man be in Christ he is a new creature. He is new by Christ's power to change him, not by the power of his own suffering.

God's work of redemption is final. God said, "I will remember your sins no more." It is possible that the memory of God should be able to blank out all memory of the sins that were once ours if we have been cleansed from them. The psalmist said: "As far as the east is from the west, so far does he remove our transgressions from us" (Ps. 103:12, RSV). If we go from north to south around the globe we can reach the South Pole and then our direction is changed as we proceed around the earth, for we are then traveling north. But if we go east around the equator, we may keep traveling east forever.

The Old Testament priest used to take a goat, in pleading forgiveness for the people. He would place his hands upon the scapegoat as if to lay the burden of the people's transgressions there. Then the priest would take the animal to a far place and release it so that it couldn't find its way back, symbolizing the carrying away of the people's sins (Lev. 16:22).

Isaiah wrote: "Though your sins be as scarlet, they shall be as white as snow." It is said that scarlet is the most difficult dye to remove from cloth, but here it is said, "Though your sins be as scarlet. . . ." They shall not be washed white by our purgatorial tears, but because God, by his own miracle, by his own gift, has washed them completely (Isa. 1:18).

Micah wrote: "Thou wilt cast all our sins into the depths of the sea." When I was studying for a Navy commission, we were instructed that our codebook was a precious item, and that if we were in danger of being captured and the secret code discovered, we should note that the codebook was bound in heavy lead. If cast into the sea it would sink to the bottom and be beyond recovery. God has recorded our sins but when we receive his forgiveness they are cast into the depths of the sea—they will not be found floating a foot below the surface to be read aloud again, once we have been redeemed and forgiven. "Who is a God like thee, pardoning iniquity and passing over transgression for the remnant of his inheritance? He does not retain his anger for ever because he delights in steadfast love. He will again have compassion upon us. . . . thou wilt cast all our sins into the depths of the sea" (Micah 7:18, 19, RSV).

Paul wrote: "There is therefore now no condemnation for those who are in Christ Jesus. For the law of the Spirit of life in Christ Jesus has set me free from the law of sin and death" (Rom. 8:1, 2, RSV).

John wrote: "My little children, I am writing this to you so that you may not sin; but if any one does sin, we have an advocate with the Father, Jesus Christ the righteous" (1 John 2:1, RSV). "Advocate" means a defense attorney—meaning that Jesus is willing to plead for us, willing to take our sins to the tribunal of God, provided that we plead guilty and throw ourselves on the mercy of the court. We should not come with a defense for our sins, with arguments about why the case should be dismissed. We must admit our guilt, confess our sins, and throw ourselves on the mercy of the court—and he will gain for us a pardon.

Christ himself has paid the debt of our sins. Dr. Francis Patton, or Princeton Theological Seminary, said, "There is not one syllable in the Bible that lends the doctrine of purgatory the least support." God's work of redemption is sufficient.

4
THE RESURRECTIONS

TWO DOCTRINES ARE NECESSARY TO salvation: the deity of Christ and the resurrection of Christ. Paul wrote: "If you confess with your lips that Jesus is Lord . . . you will be saved" (Rom. 10:9, RSV). Jesus said: "Unless you believe that I am the Messiah, the Son of God, you will die in your sins" (John 8:24, TLB). No one can be saved who does not accept Jesus as God's Son, the Messiah.

Paul's statement also showed that a belief in the resurrection was essential for salvation. He wrote: "[If you] believe in your heart that God raised him from the dead, you will be saved" (Rom. 10:9, RSV). Christ himself prophesied: "Behold, we are going up to Jerusalem; and the Son of man will be delivered to the chief priests and scribes, and they will condemn him to death, and deliver him to the Gentiles to be mocked and scourged and crucified, and he will be raised on the third day" (Matt. 20:18, 19, RSV). Believing in Jesus for salvation means believing this statement about his resurrection.

Reanimations or arousements are not resurrections. The word in Matthew for "be raised" is *egeiro*. Their bodies were revived but not changed. Lazarus, for example, was raised only to die again. He later went up to the feast at Jerusalem. His body was the same. It had just been brought back to life. John reported that many came, not to see Jesus but to see Lazarus whom he had raised from the dead. Here again the word for "raised" is *egeiro*. It was used very commonly of Jesus' miracles. In John we read: "The crowd that had been with him when he called Lazarus out of the tomb and raised him from the dead bore witness" (12:17, RSV).

The same was true at the time of Jesus' resurrection.

Matthew wrote: "the tombs also were opened, and many bodies of the saints who had fallen asleep were raised, and coming out of the tombs after his resurrection they went into the holy city and appeared to many" (27:52, 53, RSV). Probably these, as Lazarus, came forth with the same bodies—they had not become celestial bodies yet.

Jesus said to Jairus' daughter: "'Little girl, I say to you, arise.' And immediately, the girl got up and walked" (Mark 5:41, 42, RSV). The word is *egeiro* again. In the house of the ruler of the synagogue the girl walked once more in her revived body which had not been transformed, but only revived and raised.

The same was true of the son of the widow of Nain. Jesus said to the young man lying on the bier: "Young man, I say to you, arise" (Luke 7:14, RSV). The same verb is used again. He was resurrected, but not in the form of a celestial body as was Jesus' body or our future resurrection bodies will be.

JESUS RESURRECTED BODY

After his resurrection, Jesus was recognizable, so he must have had some of the same physical attributes. But in other ways, this body was different. It not only could operate normally here on earth, but it was also one that would be suited to his celestial, heavenly existence that was soon to follow. He could suddenly appear and disappear—even pass through closed doors.

The resurrection will change our mortal bodies. "We await a Savior, the Lord Jesus Christ, who will change our lowly body to be like his glorious body" (Phil. 3:20, 21, RSV). The word for change is *metaskeematizo*. The *American Standard Bible* translates it "fashion anew the body." Goodspeed's translation translated it "make our poor bodies over." *The Living Bible* translates it "take these dying bodies of ours and change them into glorious bodies like his own."

The power of all following resurrections are resident in Christ's. If Christ is not risen your faith is futile, for as all die, so in Christ shall all be made alive.

Joseph Renan, the skeptic, said, "You Christians live on the fragrance of an empty vase." That is true, for it is the glory of Christianity that the tomb was empty on the third day.

THE PROOFS OF HIS RESURRECTION

There was first of all the testimony of Christ: "I am the first and the last, and the living one; I died, and behold I am alive for evermore" (Rev. 1:17, 18, RSV). There is also the testimony of the empty tomb. The disciples saw that the tomb was empty. But how was it emptied and by whom? Some claim that the soldiers were bribed to say, "While we slept the body was stolen." If they were sleeping, how did they know what happened? Who took the body?

It was not the disciples as all except John had, in fear, run away from the crucifixion scene and were hiding out from many of the hostile people who had crucified Jesus. They were too frightened to have stolen the body.

There was the unusual condition within the tomb. When Peter and John looked into it, there was certainly none of the characteristics of what would appear to be a burglarized tomb. The napkin that was wound around his head lay folded in perfect order, and the clothes that were wrapped around the body were still in the form of a body, but the body was gone.

When a house is burglarized, usually nothing is put back in its place as the burglar is usually in a hurry. Not so with the tomb. There was no hurry or disarray—everything was orderly.

How was the stone rolled away? It is possible that it weighed more than a ton. The hands of two frightened women could not have moved it, yet the stone had been rolled away (Matt. 28:2).

If the body had been stolen, anyone who could have produced the corpse could have proven that the resurrection did not take place. But all who saw the body of Jesus Christ after the resurrection saw a living, active body, with the marks of one who had been crucified. Yet he could eat with them, drink with them, speak with them.

There was also the testimony of those who saw him after the resurrection. Paul wrote: "For I delivered to you as of first importance what I also received, that Christ died for our sins in accordance with the scriptures, that he was buried, that he was raised on the third day in accordance with the scriptures, and that he appeared to Cephas, then to the twelve. Then he appeared to more than five hundred brethren at one time, most of whom are still alive, though some have fallen asleep. Then he appeared to James, then to all the apostles" (1 Cor. 15:3-7, RSV). Now just how many witnesses does one need to establish a fact like this? Remember also that some of these people died for this testimony. Would people die for a known lie?

Paul continued: "If Christ has not been raised. . . . We are even found to be misrepresenting God [false witnesses—plain liars], because we testified of God that he raised Christ, whom he did not raise if it is true that the dead are not raised" (1 Cor. 15:14, 15, RSV).

If there was no resurrection, then there is no real Church—the body of Christ. Even a short time after the resurrection, even his disciples could not believe he was still alive. They had gone back to their nets, thinking that perhaps he in whom they had put their faith as a delivering Messiah had been destroyed on a cross and could never be seen again. They were on the sea when a voice called from the seashore, beckoning them to come and have breakfast. Suddenly, John, aboard the boat, having forsaken his Messianic call and gone back to fishing, recognized the voice, and told Peter that the voice they heard was the Lord's. Peter, half swimming, half wading, made his way directly to the Master and saw him face to face, as did the other disciples. And Christ broke bread with them and ate some of the fish. They came to know again that he was alive from the dead. Once more they left their nets and went out to follow him and once more became fishers of men. Why? Because they had seen him in the flesh. They had eaten with him and talked with him.

Again he appeared to his disciples at their meal when he "was known to them in the breaking of the bread." Perhaps his table manners and the way he said the blessing let them know he was alive again (Luke 24:35).

THE FIRST RESURRECTION OF THE SAINTS
At Christ's coming those who belong to him will be raised. "For the Lord himself will descend from heaven with a cry of command, with the archangel's call, and with the sound of the trumpet of God. And the dead in Christ will rise first; then we who are alive, who are left, shall be caught up together with them in the clouds to meet the Lord in the air; and so we shall always be

with the Lord" (1 Thess. 4:16, 17, RSV).

Those who hear his command are included in this resurrection. When I was in command of a company on maneuvers in World War I, we were marching along when an officer, of considerable rank, surprised me by calling to my men: "Company halt!"

A few men faltered for a moment, but they kept marching on. Finally the officer said to me, "Will you halt your company?"

I said, "Yes, sir," and then yelled, "Company halt!" And they all halted.

He asked to address the company, and said, "Men, that was fine! Your orders are to never take an order except from your immediate commander—it might be the enemy misrepresenting himself. Good work, men." Then he said to me, "March your company on," and I said, "Company, forward march," and they did.

Those who will hear his commands are those who have heard them here on earth, those who have made it a habit of life to obey the voice of Christ when he has spoken to them. They will hear him who have tuned their ears to the wave length of his voice. If he commands us to follow him here and we follow him, then we will hear his voice and follow him into endless days. Deaf to his voice here, we shall be deaf to his voice then—every heart must learn to hear his command on this side of the sea.

THE RESURRECTION OF THE MARTYRS

"Then I saw thrones, and seated on them were those to whom judgment was committed. Also I saw the souls of those who had been beheaded for their testimony to

Jesus and for the word of God, and who had not worshiped the beast or its image and had not received its mark on their foreheads or their hands. They came to life, and reigned with Christ a thousand years. The rest of the dead did not come to life until the thousand years were ended. This is the first resurrection'' (Rev. 20:4, 5, RSV).

We can read something of the courage of these in Hebrews 11. They typify the courage of so many in the great challenges of today as we think of those who are willing to lay down their lives for him.

THE NATURE OF THE RESURRECTED BODY

This important question is presented to us by Paul who wrote: "But some one will ask, 'How are the dead raised? With what kind of body do they come?'" (1 Cor. 15:35, RSV). There are two opinions as to the nature of the resurrection body.

It will be the same body, some say. Certain Bible interpreters believe that the same particles of the body will be reunited—that the Creator has the power to reassemble the atoms which composed our earthly body.

This idea may seem extreme and grotesque to some people. They would prefer to give to the great Designer power to do what he will about the details of how this body might be reformed.

It will be similar to our earthly body, others say. It will be like our original body but not identical. Some believe that the cells within the human body almost completely change at least every seven years—some faster, some slower. The entire body, though it changes in this way, except for the teeth, maintains a certain similarity that is recognizable from year to year. We can still recognize people we haven't seen for over thirty years or longer.

The resurrection body will be, first of all, a changed body that will be like Christ's resurrection body. Paul said that there is a terrestrial (earthly) body and also a celestial (heavenly) body. "But the glory of the celestial is one, and the glory of the terrestrial is another" (1 Cor. 15:40, RSV). So it is with the resurrection of the dead. What is sown (buried) is perishable. What is raised is imperishable, but there is a similarity. Paul went on to say that if one sows a wheat seed in the ground it perishes in the sense that the seed disintegrates, and yet that seed gives life to wheat. If one sows barley seed he will have a harvest of barley—not oats or wheat. When our body is buried and is raised again, it will be our body, not another's. It will be a body fit for heavenly existence as our earthly body was built for earthly existence. "It is sown a physical body, it is raised a spiritual body" (v. 44) fashioned for heaven.

It will be a deathless body. What is raised is imperishable. There is no death in heaven. All suffering fades and illness and death are eliminated, so we will not be the victims of any disease or threatening handicaps.

Note the further changes indicated in 1 Corinthians 15:

It is sown:	*It is raised:*
In corruption	In incorruption
In dishonor	In glory
In weakness	In power
Natural, earthly	Heavenly, spiritual

Some wonder if it will be a sexless body. We do not know, but of course there is no need for procreation in heaven.

Jesus said, "They neither marry nor are given in marriage, but are like angels" (Matt. 22:30, RSV). There need be no births in heaven because there are no deaths; so some feel there are no marital relationships carried over into the heavenly existence.

We are told that our celestial bodies will be like Christ's resurrected body. Paul wrote: "But our commonwealth is in heaven, and from it we await a Savior, the Lord Jesus Christ, who will change our lowly body to be like his glorious body, by the power which enables him even to subject all things to himself" (Phil. 3:20, 21, RSV). Jesus has power to recreate our bodies to be like his own.

Notice the characteristics of Christ's resurrected body. It was definitely a physical body. He was seen by many. He appeared to Mary Magdalene physically in the garden. She went to him and wanted to hold onto him as though to delay him, and he asked her not to touch him or cling to him. Soon after, in Luke 24, he sat at dinner with the men and "was known to them in the breaking of the bread."

According to Paul, more than five hundred saw him at one time. He was not only visible but physical. "As they were saying this, Jesus himself stood among them. But they were startled and frightened, and supposed they saw a spirit [ghost]. And he said to them, 'Why are you troubled, and why do questionings rise in your hearts? See my hands and my feet, that it is I myself; handle me, and see; for a spirit has not flesh and bones as you see that I have'" (Luke 24:36-40, RSV). This passage certainly gives no place for the theory of a mere spiritual manifestation of Jesus as the only result of the resurrection. He asked them to use their senses of touching, seeing, feeling to prove that he was physically alive and present.

He had an audible voice and the power of hearing. The physical senses of sight and sound were there. He was perfectly willing to have people touch him for the proof they needed of his physical resurrection.

To doubt the resurrection is to doubt the Lord himself. To doubt our eventual resurrection is to doubt that he was raised from the dead, or that he was the Son of God as he claimed. On these truths rest all our faith.

5
THE JUDGMENTS

THE IDEA OF JUDGMENT IS ALMOST universal. Even primitive tribes embrace some system of justice. Just laws among mankind seem to have been vital to the preservation of the animal kingdom, trees and plants, and all of human existence as well. The earliest people had their laws and councils to enforce even crude systems of reward and punishment.

There were the laws of Hammurabi in the early days. The Ten Commandments were given to the Jews at the beginning of their national history. Greece had its systems of ethics and its social order. Rome had its system of jurisprudence.

What nation today would think of dismissing all of its judges? A healthy society demands of its judges good character and fairness. People know that there is punishment for killing, rape, slander, theft, and violence or soon the nation would sink into an immoral morass and man would soon cry out again for law and order.

The great religions of the world all embody some kind of judgment. The Moslems have their Koran with its restrictive codes; Judaism has its Talmud. The Shintoists have their own codes. The Bible was written to give the laws and standards of God.

WHO IS THE JUDGE?

It is also fundamental to Christianity and the Scriptures that judgment is a part of life. The words "judgment, judging, judges," occur over seven hundred times in Scripture. In Christian theology, Christ himself is the Judge. "He [God] hath appointed a day, in the which he will judge the world in righteousness by that man whom he hath ordained [appointed]; whereof he hath given assurance unto all men, in that he hath raised him [Christ] from the dead" (Acts. 17:31). The meaning of Easter is that by this act of the resurrection, God himself has put the imprimatur of judgeship upon his Son, Jesus Christ. "God shall bring every work into judgment, with every secret thing, whether it be good, or whether it be evil" (Eccl. 12:14).

Paul wrote: "For we must all appear before the judgment seat of Christ" (2 Cor. 5:10). Christ also spoke about his office as judge: "When the Son of man shall come in his glory . . . then shall he sit upon the throne of his glory: and before him shall be gathered all nations: and he shall separate them one from another, as a shepherd divideth his sheep from the goats" (Matt. 25:31, 32).

God has handed the task of judging over to his Son. "The Father judges no one, but has given all judgment to the Son, that all may honor the Son, even as they honor the Father" (John 5:22, 23, RSV). I am glad that Christ is to be the judge of mankind, because that assures us of an understanding on the part of this Judge. He knows our frame. He knows our hearts.

THE ASSURANCES

Christ's reactions concerning us are not founded upon a lack of understanding or a misjudgment, however frequent these things may be true of us.

A man on a Pullman car had with him in his berth a very young child who was crying and whimpering constantly. Naturally it kept many people on the train awake. Finally, one man in a neighboring berth pulled his curtain aside, and said angrily, "Why don't you bring that little brat to his mother?"

The man holding the child said, "I wish I could, sir, but right now his mother lies in a casket in the baggage car." How often we misjudge situations and people! But not Christ.

Christ's judgeship also assures us of an understanding of how powerful temptation can be. Christ was led by the Spirit into the wilderness to be tempted by the devil, but he won over every form of the temptation.

The writer of Hebrews reminded us that "we have not a high priest who is unable to sympathize with our weaknesses" (Heb. 4:15, RSV). Every passionate longing and desire that surges through us surged through him as well. He was "one who in every respect has been tempted as we are, yet without sin" (4:15, RSV). He does not ask us to walk any path that he has not walked himself and he knows the pressures of life. He was angry when some of the people refused to believe. How righteously indignant he must have felt when hanging on a cross knowing that, as one of the thieves said, he was guilty of no unrighteousness. How indignant he could have felt toward the centurion that had him scourged. How easy it would have been to fall prey to the temptation of turning his back on the price of our redemption and going back to heaven. He was offered infinite political power if he would only fall down and compromise with Satan and his empire.

Jesus as judge is always leaning toward mercy and clemency. It is not his will that any should perish, but that all should come to the truth.

Some say, "But is not this idea of judgment and punishment contrary to the nature of a God who is love?" No. Take a coin and hold it toward the sun. The part which is turned toward the sun is glistening, showing forth its brilliance. But look at the side of the coin which is turned away from the sun. It is in the shadows and dark. That is a law of physics—you cannot change it. This is true of a human soul, nature, and character.

When our hearts are turned toward God in the desire to see his will and know his will and do his will, God's pleasure is shining down upon us. But if our hearts are woefully turned away from God in willful disobedience and arrogance, then it is a law of spiritual life that we are standing in the shadow and in the darkness of his anger. God receives all those who will turn and come to him. "Him who comes to me I will not cast out" (John 6:37, RSV).

JUDGMENTS OF THE CROSS

A preliminary hearing began at the cross. We know we can bring ourselves to Christ, with our transgressions, our problems, and our possible condemnation at any time upon any day. A person is put on trial usually just once for an offense. If I am fined for speeding or breaking some other statute of the vehicle code, it is possible for me to settle that case almost immediately. I may go down to the clerk of the court and plead guilty to the charge. The court may tell me what the fine is and I may pay that fine and immediately the case is closed. My name is taken off the docket. Never again will my name come up in court for that same offense, because from then on there is no condemnation against me for that wrong. I have taken care of it.

You and I need not wait for the judgment of the great white throne. John wrote, "If any man sin, we have an advocate [a defense attorney]" (1 John 2:1). If we confess our sins to him—throw ourselves on the mercy of the court—he will give us not a dismissal but a pardon on the basis of our having pleaded guilty. He himself has paid the price by the gift of himself on the cross. Paul said that where we stand now there is no condemnation for them that are in Christ, for we have already passed from death unto life.

Our case was heard at the cross and the price paid for our sins. Our names are taken from the roll of the guilty. That is why we are supposed to pray daily to God, "Forgive us our debts, as we forgive our debtors." This daily forgiveness requested then takes place every day, and at the end of any day our records can be wiped clean. This is our daily personal judgment of ourselves, "But if we judged ourselves truly [honestly], we should not be judged" (1 Cor. 11:31, RSV).

THE JUDGMENT OF THE NATIONS

I saw a fascinating picture of God one day. It showed him as a man sitting, playing chess. On the chessboard were the various nations of the world. God has one aim and purpose, that his will be done on earth as it is in heaven. As the nations helped him in forming the kind of world he desired with fraternity, goodness, peace, and love, they remained on the board of history. But as soon as they so conducted themselves as to get in the way of his plan and purpose, they were taken from the board of history. This is not so much a trial of persons as a trial of collective nations.

Remember how God in Christ functioned on the judgment seat of history. He is not there just to condemn but also to commend what nations are doing. The Greek emphasis on the word, "judge" is *kritees,* or *krisis.*

These words for judge have a negative connotation. He is there to judge and condemn, and there such a judge sits ready to condemn nations rather than to commend them. Here the word can mean not only to punish but to praise, but the usual emphasis is on condemnation.

The Hebrew idea of the judge in many situations is more merciful. The word used for judge was sometimes *shofet-shafet-mishpet.* This is a richer and more positive idea of God as a judge than was the Greek. We read "For God sent the Son into the world, not to condemn the world, but that the world might be saved through him" (John 3:17, RSV). Christ came not to destroy but to save mankind, not to tear down the nations but to establish a new order among them. Christ admonished us to pray: "Thy kingdom come, thy will be done, on earth as it is in heaven" (Matt. 6:10, RSV). Israel understood a judge to be someone whose duty it was to punish and pass sentence when laws had been broken willfully. But often his office had little to do with jurisprudence. He was one who had come to advise, to point out constructively the things that were troubling nations and people, explaining how, in Jehovah's sight they were going astray. How anxious Jehovah was to adjust to justice and to help rehabilitate persons and nations!

God censured their failures to deliver the poor out of the oppression by the enemy and taught them how they might come to the proper state of mind and purpose. Before God punished Pharaoh by sending the plagues, he warned him many times.

Jehovah patiently counseled with Israel as to his reason for bringing her to such a high estate—he gave her the commandments, the prophets, victory in battle, and stature in the world. He did these things to make them a light to the Gentiles. The Jews were his missionaries who were to go to tell them that Jehovah was the Lord God.

I have seen many human illustrations of the nature of God—as leader of his army, as Creator of the universe, as the Father of all mankind, as a kindly Father, guiding his children. But I think the most unique and fitting illustration I saw was the painting of him as the man playing chess.

America should remember that God is the Judge of nations. There was a reason for God to raise up America, coddling her as a child from her beginning, for sending the Pilgrim fathers to her with one aim and purpose in their minds: "to build a kingdom of their Lord and Savior, Jesus Christ." This they tried to do. They built their churches, they put God in education, and fashioned most of their laws to what they perceived to be the mind of God. They loved the Lord's day, they worshiped faithfully in their churches.

The teachers of America's first universities were clergymen or Christian men. God was on their campuses. Our fathers desired no independence apart from Jehovah God. America, in its constitution and in its laws, desired to become a nation under God, which would mean a nation never under the yoke of bondage to another man.

If we forsake this aim and purpose, we should prepare to see America removed from the chessboard of history and to some other nation displacing it in power and importance.

In a day when crime is rampant, when drunkenness and violence find a new high, when the Lord's day is honored only by a few, when God's laws are ignored, then we should take care lest God's judgment of the nations be repeated in his judgment of America.

There is something very special about this judgment of the nations. God has reminded us that "If my people who are called by my name humble themselves, and pray and . . . turn from their wicked ways, then will I . . . heal their land" (2 Chron. 7:14, RSV).

When we serve God we do it through service to his people. The only way we can bless God is by blessing his children. Our habitation in heaven is going to be judged in some degree by our rehabilitation of his needy children here on earth. Heaven will be made up of those who have learned to care.

On several trips abroad, I have seen what America has done for other nations—the orphanages she has built, the hospitals, the factories, the diseases she has wiped out, the protection she has offered to the defenseless, and the succor she has given the world in foreign aid. It made me proud to be an American. On countless occasions I prayed that I might be worthy of being a member of a nation that cared for others. Only a nation that saves is worth saving. I can well understand what Winston Churchill said, "You can say what you want about America, in spite of her weaknesses and her mistakes, the universe has never known a more unselfish, kind nation than the United States."

THE JUDGMENT OF SATAN

We cannot read much of the Bible without coming to the conclusion that God has permitted the existence of opposition to his rule on earth.

Many think that we have a vision of Satan's origin in Ezekiel 28 where he is described as a cherub nearest to the mercy seat in the presence of Almighty God. Here he coveted the power and position of God and for his insubordination was cast out of heaven and departed with those who would follow him. Satan is a Hebrew word denoting "adversary, an enemy, an accuser." Satan and the devil are the same personality. Throughout the Scriptures the outstanding enemy is Satan, seen as a serpent—tempting and disobedient. In Job he is seen falsely accusing the man of God, tempting him, punishing him, depriving him of home, and family, and fortune, trying to prove to Jehovah that no person would love God for God's own sake.

In the New Testament, we see Satan trying to build his own empire of evil. We see Christ led up into the wilderness to be tempted by the devil. We see the prince of darkness—the prince of this world, come into fierce spiritual conflict with Christ, the Prince of Heaven and the Prince of Light. The story of the Kingdom of God from then on becomes largely one of conflict between these two princes. Christ prayed that Satan would not win Peter in the conflict between the two and that Peter would be able to stand. Pentecost demonstrated that Christ won the battle.

Satan tried to defeat Christ's purposes at the cross. Satan put it in the heart of Judas to betray his Lord. Satan, the devil in the New Testament, is constantly busy trying to undermine the Church. It is he who caused Ananias and Sapphira to lie to the Holy Ghost (Acts 5).

The names given to Satan are most graphic and cunning. He is called *antidikos* ("adversary") and *diabolos* ("devil") in 1 Peter 5:8. In Matthew 12, he is called *Beelzebub,* the prince of devils. In Revelation 12:10 he is the accuser. He is called the dragon (Rev. 12:7). Elsewhere he is called *Lucifer,* meaning "light bearer" (Isa. 14:12).

Christ warned his people about the subtleties of the devil. He would come as an angel of light—not something with a forked tail and pitchfork, but an attractive, convincing, personality who would sometimes deceive even the Lord's elect. He would also lead the synagogue of Satan—the false church. Many would follow him despite Christ's warning of his subtle wiles. Only Christ's power could cast out the demons, which have been placed in human hearts by Satan, the chief of demons.

Christ's disciples came to him to report: "We saw the devils cast out." They saw that men could be changed.

"I saw Satan falling like fire from heaven," Jesus replied.

When Christ foretold his death, what might have seemed to be defeat, he cried out, "Father, glorify thy name." Then came a voice from heaven saying, "I have glorified it, and I will glorify it again" (John 12:28, RSV). And the people stood by and heard it; some thought it sounded like thunder, and others said that an angel had spoken to him. Jesus answered and said, "This voice has come for your sake, not for mine. Now is the judgment of this world, now shall the ruler of this world be cast out, and I, when I am lifted up from the earth, will draw all men to myself" (12:30-32, RSV).

Christ will conquer. Satan will be overcome and cast out. Christ will sit upon the throne, as King of kings, and Lord of lords.

We have come to one of these mountain peaks—the judgment of the resurrection in Revelation 20, the judgment of the great white throne, and the final victory of Christ over the hosts of darkness. "And when the thousand years are ended, Satan will be loosed from his prison and will come out to deceive the nations which are at the four corners of the earth, that is, Gog and Magog, to gather them for battle; their number is like the sand of the sea" (Rev. 20:7, 8, RSV).

How literal is that picture that follows in Revelation 20? Some difficulties pointed out in making this a literal picture are the problem of geography. How, for example could billions possibly be gathered together in a single place?

There is also the problem of literal time. How can we expect millions of people to be put on trial? How could their cases be heard even though the review of their deeds be hasty? How could it be decided in an hour of final judgment whether or not our names should be written in the book of life—guaranteeing us eternal life? But we believe God is judging us all the time. By the time we reach the point of death, our standing in this day of judgment is fixed. God has already determined whether or not we are worthy of having our names written. This judgment is evidently not a time for examination and cross-examination and the presentation of personal evidence for every individual. It is merely the report of God as to whether or not our names are written in the book of life. It will be a time when he will separate the sheep from the goats and announce whose is the gift of eternal life.

THE JUDGMENT SEAT OF CHRIST

It was the custom in Rome for Caesar to preside at two kinds of judgments or trials. One was the trial which ended in a decision of life or death, determining whether a person was worthy of flogging, imprisonment, execution by beheading, crucifixion, or death in the arena. Caesar had to judge between guilt and innocence. The other legal session, the *bema,* was a tribunal —not of judgments, but for awards. It was this session with the populace that Caesar loved. At this time he was happy to present to a faithful mother a coin embossed with the likeness of his head because of her faithful service rendered in love and faithfulness. Here, the athlete received his crown of olive leaves to celebrate his victory in the games. There was an award for a soldier who had fought valiantly in battle for Rome and for her glory. This was the judgment of awards.

The Christian is to enjoy such a court of awards. It will be when we are gathered before Christ, not for condemnation, but for commendation, for we must all stand before the judgment seat of Christ to receive the rewards for what we did on earth. There will be varying degrees of honor, and perhaps some remorse because at that time we will also probably be conscious of our omissions in life.

It is altogether possible that Paul had never forgotten how in the stoning of Christian Stephen, he had joined in that display of brutality by "holding their coats" while they were stoning this man of God. Probably he never forgot how Stephen's anguished face was lifted to God and how his voice was not calling for revenge, nor showing hatred toward those who were killing him, and how he had pleaded that God should not lay this sin to their charge. Someone in a poem pictured Paul, rather dreading the day when he would meet Stephen face to face and ask for his forgiveness for that dark hour. Paul, as he recalls his arrest of Christians, bringing them to unjust punishment because of their faith in Christ was, in the poem, saying:

Saints did I say—your well-remembered faces,
Dear men and women whom I sought and slew;
O when we meet in heaven's places—
How shall I weep to Stephen and to you!

It is possible that on that day Christ will thank us for our part in missionary zeal. Queen Victoria was once asked how long it would take her army and navy to get a message from her around the world. She said she thought they could do it in about two years. Jesus Christ, our King, commanded us to go in all the world and preach the gospel to every creature. Two thousand years have passed and perhaps a third of the world has not even heard of the gospel.

We know that our walk must be upright. We know we are saved by faith, but yet faith without works is dead. Paul reminded us that we are saved by grace, through faith in Jesus Christ, but he also stated that we are saved for good works.

It is reasonable that while salvation is for all who earnestly believe and serve him, that there be a difference of awards in the final judgment of his kingdom.

It is hardly fair to say that the thief on the cross, who gave to Christ only one hour of faithfulness, should receive the same reward as Timothy who, from a child, had known the Scriptures and had served Christ faithfully in his church until his death.

Would the man who waited until he had his second heart attack before he came to Christ receive exactly the same award as one who had given him a life of tireless service? We have seen and noted that the martyrs who gave their lives in service and sacrifice to Jesus Christ have a part in the first resurrection where they are paid special honors.

We know how difficult it is to lead Christian lives in a society as decadent as ours today without suffering some form of persecution from those about us. They might not scourge us as was done in Rome, but they will scorn us. They might not lash us with thongs, but they will laugh at us. They might not cast us out, as early Christians were, to freeze to death on the ice floes, but they will freeze us to death in society.

At this final judgment seat, Christ might say, for example, to Peter and John, who were threatened by death by the godless mob, "Because you were willing to suffer with me, you shall reign with me." May it be said of all of us.

6
*HELL—
THE ABODE OF
THE WICKED*

FRANKLY, I WISH THIS SUBJECT WERE NOT a part of the future. It would be easier for me to just skip it, evade it, explain it away, or try to deny it. I don't think we could honestly do any of these, because the reward of good must be properly balanced with the punishment of evil. We cannot accept one without accepting both because the Bible teaches both. The side of an object turned toward the sun is in the light. The side turned from it is in the darkness. Lives obediently turned toward God enjoy the smile of God. Those turned away from him in rebellion suffer the anger of God. God's physical laws and spiritual laws are fixed and reliable.

Why then, one may ask, do many people oppose the doctrine of hell? To many, hell is an embarrassing and unpleasant subject. "Why drag a skeleton into the pleasant banquet hall?" they ask. Some books on eschatology omit it, or pass it by so quickly that they might as well have skipped it. Some churches don't preach about hell to avoid being called "brimstone corner." Others gladly preach the love of God but weakly neglect teaching about the justice of God.

Others oppose the idea of hell because it is so often overemphasized and glamorized. Michelangelo's "Last Judgment" in the Sistine Chapel in Rome, pictured in the center Christ, the irate Judge, in a gesture of retribution. Demons lie at his feet, faces twisted in despair. Martyrs are seemingly enjoying and encouraging Christ to avenge them. Mary, at his right hand, is turning her face away from the horror.

Tertullian also pictured the saints being comforted by seeing the agony of their persecutors. A Dutch confession states: "The pious will see the terrible revenge which God will take on the godless who have tyrannized, persecuted, and tortured them in this world." It is possible that Paul's words to suffering saints was interpreted to mean that judgment on the evil would bring comfort to the persecuted: "God will give you rest along with us when the Lord Jesus appears suddenly from heaven in flaming fire with his mighty angels, bringing judgment . . ." (2 Thess. 1:7, 8, TLB). It is more likely that Paul was referring to the comfort of being rescued rather than from seeing judgment come to the persecutors.

The doctrine of hell is laughed at by others. They make light of the idea that God would take sin so seriously. They prefer to believe that God in his patience might be willing to ignore sin or to tolerate it and that in spite of our attitude, he will simply forget our transgressions even without our repentance. Some preachers overload the subject. Others overlook it altogether. One pastor said that he had never preached on the subject of hell and never would.

Christ mentioned hell, or its equivalent, many times in his teaching. Paul, James, Peter, and John all mentioned it in their writings. The business of an ambassador is to deliver the message of his government, not deny it, change it, or invent other messages. So it is with his messengers today.

May we never be guilty of an imbalance in our messages. Let us see to it that the picture given us of hell and of God's hatred of sin hangs far below the picture of Christ on the cross, paying the price for our sins.

God's chief desire is that we choose heaven—not hell. It is not the will of God that any should perish. He prepared heaven for us. Hell was planned for the devil and his angels. But if we insist upon following the devil, there is nothing God will do but let us go with him. Hell is simply God's surrender to man's refusal to accept God's salvation, and man being endowed with free will, there is no more that God will do.

Should God take away our ability to decide, we would no longer be made in his image. If God ever seems to be, or is far off, it was we who strayed away—not God, for he never changes.

MOST RELIGIONS BELIEVE IN TWO PLACES

It seems evident that God has put instinctively in the human mind the reasonableness of a belief in a heaven and a hell. The Greeks called the place of punishment *tartaros* (Tartarus), which is a place of torture by hunger and thirst, with water just out of reach. Indian Veda religion knows there is a hell. Islam believes it. Buddhism embraces the idea of a place of punishment. Judaism talks about Sheol and its pangs of memory. Jesus mentioned Gehenna, or the Valley of Hinnom from which it derived its name, eleven times. The Valley of Hinnom was figuratively the place of broken and discarded things, a refuse heap.

FUTURE JUSTICE—A DETERRENT TO CRIME

Ruskin said, "The denial of hell is the most damaging thing because it is the most attractive form of infidelity."

The chaplain of a large penitentiary said, "Many have been affected by this doctrine. Nothing could uphold them in crime at the risk of life, like this denial."

A well-known judge reinforced this conviction by saying: "Were all preachers not to preach this doctrine [of hell] there would be all hell in this world if not in the next." When some theologians and psychologists call hell a laughing matter and call a sense of guilt and sin just a "neurosis," they are doing their generation a serious disservice.

One of our leading denominational journals wrote some time ago: "Some who deny hell might just be calling Christ a liar and unwittingly be making their own bed in hell and are not smart enough to see it."

ARGUMENTS AGAINST HELL

Some prefer that the wicked in the end finally perish and be no more—annihilation, as we discussed earlier. They quote Paul: "For many, of whom I have often told you and now tell you even with tears, live as enemies of the cross of Christ. Their end is destruction, their god is the belly, and they glory in their shame, with minds set on earthly things" (Phil. 3:18, 19, RSV).

They also quote Peter: "And especially those who indulge in the lust of defiling passion and despise authority. Bold and wilful, they are not afraid to revile the glorious ones . . . in matters of which they are ignorant, will be destroyed in the same destruction with them, suffering wrong for their wrongdoing" (2 Peter 2:10-13, RSV).

But the Scriptures say that all the wicked will be raised in a general resurrection to stand trial, so these promises of destruction are obviously not talking about a final and complete annihilation. John wrote: "I saw the dead, great and small, standing before the throne" (Rev. 20:12, RSV). None escaped that after-death hearing. The soul of man is indestructible. We are to be forever with the Lord or forever without him. The word "eternal" is used of both heaven and hell. There is a certain time limit to our chance of life and our opportunity to repent, this choice to be made before our death. Death does not change us—it fixes us. It is in this life that we set the rudder in the direction in which we forever sail.

But some say, "I will depend upon the goodness of God to allow a man to change his mind after death." They cite the verse that says that at the return of Christ "in the twinkling of an eye we shall all be changed" (1 Cor. 15:52). But this is not speaking of the soul—but of the human body. The Scriptures say "he which is filthy, let him be filthy still: and he that is righteous, let him be righteous still (Rev. 22:11). If we desire to be righteous and in the will of God, after death we will be more righteous, for then "we shall be like him." Let us be sure that our eyes are fixed upon Christ, that the rudder of our lives has been set in the direction of his righteousness.

God has permitted us, of our own free will, to do that. Christ couched his deepest desire in his priestly prayer recorded in John 17: "Father, I will that they also, whom thou hast given me, be with me where I am; that they may behold my glory" (17:24). So, in the future, if God should be far away, we know who it was that moved.

"HELL, INC." is the name of an organization in Las Vegas, Nevada, which operates day and night, twenty-four hours every day of the week, and features every evil type of amusement and vice that exists. On the front of the building is a large five-thousand-dollar neon sign in the form of a devil, whose pitchfork arrow points the way to "Hell." Along the road between Los Angeles and Las Vegas are large road signs such as

"You're on the way to Hell," and "This is the way to Hell," or "Hell is Fun," and others. What a deplorable reflection on the spiritual condition of America! One of the devil's preoccupations is to keep us busy with the past and the future and to weaken us in the present to the real horrors of what hell is.

WHAT IS HELL?

Some say hell is just a condition—not a place—a state of feeling separated from God. Hades is where spirits dwell without a body. Hell is a condition of awareness, torment, and loneliness.

Others say it is definitely a place. Peter wrote "He [Christ] went and preached to the spirits in prison who disobeyed long ago when God waited patiently in the days of Noah" (1 Pet. 3:19, 20, NIV). Here Christ is described as speaking to people in a specific place. In this place they are said to await the resurrection and judgment.

Another word for Hades is "Gehenna," associated with the Valley of Hinnom, just outside Jerusalem, which was a junk heap. There they cast things that did not work—a mirror that had cracked, a kettle that had rusted out, broken tools, broken chariot wheels, pieces of broken pottery. Symbolically, the Valley of Hinnom, or Gehenna, was the place for persons who had suffered dissipation, drunkenness, gross sinfulness. Those who allowed truth to collapse into a lie or to whom faith had lost its sight; whose moral courage had collapsed; whose marriage vows had been broken without sufficient reason; whose inner temples of worship had crumbled under the pressures of selfish pleasures and preoccupation; whose homes had been smashed by selfishness—these were those destined for Gehenna.

These are the lives that a just God surveyed in all fairness and about which he simply could not say, "Well done, good and faithful servant." Gehenna was the dumping ground of lives that broke faith with both God and men.

Notice some of the characteristics of hell. Some of the symbols that are used are obviously less strong than the reality. It is called a "lake of fire." Some say this is literal fire. Others say it is symbolic. The rich man (Luke 16) lifted up his eyes and said, "I am tormented in these flames."

Hell is said to be a place of darkness. Peter wrote "God spared not the angels that sinned, but cast them down to hell, and delivered them into chains of darkness" (2 Peter 2:4). This darkness is perhaps the darkness of unbelief. It is a dark future that gropes blindly, not seeing the path ahead.

Christ, on the other hand, said, "I am the light of the world: he that followeth me shall not walk in darkness" (John 8:12). The darkness is missing God, his peace, his comfort, his guidance, assurance, and the knowledge of the future.

Some think that it is possible to understand something of the future by learning from those on the brink of death. A number of reports have been given about the events surrounding the dead and dying. Some are said to actually pass, at the moment of their death, into a state of consciousness entirely different from life on earth and are able to relate what they discovered.

Many accounts have been given recently, apart from

any religious convictions, faith, previous information, teaching, or biblical sources of revelation. At the time of death, when these people were thought to be slipping away, they experienced a place of beatific light and splendor, ecstatic music, warm friendships, and the sensation of walking through a tunnel of light. In the majority of such cases, the experience has been one of pleasant surprise and security. Such reports have emboldened even unbelievers.

Other physicians, nurses, and attending loved ones have recorded the very opposite reports of others as they were dying. At random and from a host of books, from a great variety of testimonies, the scene at death has been one of a tragic existence, a long dark tunnel leading to a dark area where people were in despair. Another, realizing he was dying slowly from cancer, secured from his attending physician assurance that medical sedation would be present to insure him a fearless departure.

Another claimed he was being pursued along a lake of fire, with scorching heat, and of his trying to escape from crawling things that would draw him toward the burning lake. He reported the extended helping arm of a kindly figure of light, but he was unable to take it. It was too late. Morticians have reported the stamp of tragic terror on the faces of some who died.

When I was a boy, my father, who had helped in a rescue mission, had been inviting a painter, patiently and repeatedly, to accept Christ. His invitation was refused repeatedly.

"Maybe tomorrow, maybe tomorrow," the painter would say. Late one afternoon he had fallen from a ladder, fractured his skull, and lay dying. Gasping, he said to my father in a tone of dismal horror: "Tell everyone you meet that tomorrow is the devil's lie." With a final look of despair, he was gone.

Voltaire is considered by many to be an outstanding man of literature and theater. At ten years of age he was sent to a Jesuit school and remained until he was seventeen. There, under his instructors, he came to have an intense interest in both literature and philosophy and showed great aptitude as a playwright. After producing many plays and critiques, many of which were satirical, he was the object of approbation and praise on one hand and of spirited criticism and opposition on the other.

Some of his works evidenced his strong antireligious or at least antiecclesiastical stance, and he did not hesitate to ridicule the Bible or the church. He seemed to show a growing animosity toward Christ and the Christian faith which he only partially concealed.

Several historic sources report the dismal and pathetic agony of soul and mind that possessed Voltaire when enduring the severe stroke which terminated in his death. He was immersed in remorse and desired to talk with a priest to become reconciled to the church and the Christian faith.

The companions who had praised his infidelity had feared this reconciliation and carefully guarded the sick room to keep him from verbally recanting his unbelief and opposition to the faith. Sensing this, Voltaire, in inner and outward rage, cursed them openly and their very presence incensed him, and he repeatedly cried out, "Begone, it is you that have brought me to my present condition. Leave me, I say—begone! What a wretched glory is this which you have produced for me!"

Voltaire had prepared a written recantation, which

he signed and had witnessed. Not even this brought him comfort nor alleviated his mental anguish during two months of torture. At times he would gnash his teeth and fly into uncontrolled rage against God and mankind. He would also cry out imploringly, "O, Christ! O Lord Jesus" and add in agony, "I must die abandoned of God and man." As death drew near, his situation was so frightful that his unbelieving friends dared not even approach his bedside. They stood guard at the door lest others witness the awful tragedy of an infidel about to die.

His nurse said, "For all the wealth in the world, I would never be willing to nurse another infidel."

What a tragedy when one comes to the end of the road, though endowed with great intellect, educational diplomas, a superfluity of material things, and great earthly honor—and then allow all that honor to end in horror!

We have more reliable evidence for our future salvation and dwelling place than these after-death utterances or experiences. Doctors tell us often that when the brain is robbed of circulation for a mere few minutes that disintegration sets in, causing irregular brain and thought patterns. We should approach death with a light heart, knowing that when Christ has become our Light, we will pass triumphantly through the doors of death into everlasting life. We need not depend on the utterances of dying people to understand the glorious future awaiting us.

For those who would like to pursue this problem of the experiences of unbelievers as opposed to believers at the point of death, I would strongly refer you to the book by Maurice Rawlings, M.D.: *Beyond Death's Door* (Des Plaines, IL: Bantam, 1979).

OUT OF PLACE IN HEAVEN

Some would be uneasy and out of place in heaven. Christ is said to be on the throne there as King and Lord. Never having admitted his divinity or deity here on earth, some people might be ill at ease in his presence there. How could they honestly kneel in worship of him. The Scriptures say that nothing that defiles or is immoral has a place there. Some find their delight in off-color stories, the inordinate joke, the X-rated shows. To them the pure and undefiled would be dull and boring. Some people simply do not fit in heaven.

Would a kidnapper, for instance, be placed in the same heaven as the Lindberg baby? Would the two university coeds who were raped and killed be in the same heaven as the two perverts who slew them?

Worship is mentioned twenty-three times in Revelation alone. In heaven people will worship God. The angels, the four and twenty elders, and the great multitudes sing his praises. We have been commanded to assemble together regularly and to enter his courts with praise, but some have always been frankly bored with services of worship. How ill at ease some would be with unhurried praise.

In Revelation we read that people serve him day and night in his temple (7:15). On earth we hear some saying "Oh, no! Not again! They were always trying to harness me to some task in the church." Up there it will be day and night service. Some might say, "No, thank you."

God lists some who are actually barred from heaven because they would destroy the joys of God's people: "Don't you know that those doing such things have no share in the Kingdom of God? Don't fool yourselves.

Those who live immoral lives, who are idol worshipers, adulterers or homosexuals—will have no share in his kingdom. Neither will thieves or greedy people, drunkards, slanderers, or robbers" (1 Cor. 6:9, 10, TLB). Such people could make a hell out of heaven. God loves people too much to allow that to happen.

Some people face the doctrine of hell with disbelief. They have a definite theological prejudice against it. There is the story of a man who, when dying, said, "I'll give a hundred thousand dollars to anyone who will prove there is no hell." Many like him simply don't want to believe in it.

OBJECTIONS TO THE BELIEF

Hell is inconsistent with the power of God, some say. They claim that God is powerful enough to force people to change their minds. But the moment God made man in his image, he gave him the power to make his own decisions, to do as he willed, to obey or disobey God. But the moment God takes away that power, man is no longer made in God's image—he is a puppet, a slave, unable to make a decision. God did not choose to have fellowship with robots, but with men with free will.

Hell is inconsistent with a loving God, others say. Only a cruel God would fashion such a place as hell, they reason.

"A cruel God?" we reply. For thousands of years, through his prophets, God sent forth his plan for eternal life—a Messiah to save his people. These people stoned the prophets. He sent his only Son and they persecuted him and put him to death. But the wooing would continue, for before his death, Christ promised the coming of the Holy Spirit who would testify about him.

"A cruel God?" we reply. The Holy Spirit descended and filled the people with power and love and a knowledge of God's presence—and still people would not believe, but killed those whom he sent.

"An impersonal God?" God in the Old Testament wooed people for thousands of years through his prophets who gave them laws and invited them to come to God.

"A cruel heavenly Father?" He so loved us that he gave his only begotten Son.

"An indifferent God?" He sent the Holy Spirit who came to woo and comfort and guide us and fill us with his power and reveal to us the things God has prepared for those who love him. Who, like the loving "Hound of Heaven," relentlessly pursues us to bring us home again?

God gave us ministers, evangelists, preachers to invite us, missionaries to seek us out, writers and printers to persuade us, a built-in conscience to convince us, some dedicated radio and television ministries which daily and nightly invite us into the privileges of God's people, and thousands of believing, practicing Christians who demonstrate daily the power of God in their lives.

In our stupid rebellion we fall into the well of our wandering from God. Constantly God lowers down the ladder of his love, but we refuse to raise ourselves. We even push away the downward reaching hand of the Father—we refuse the pierced hand of the Son of God and are deaf to the cry of the Holy Spirit who pleads "Come."

How could anyone say God is not concerned about

us? "How shall we escape, if we neglect so great salvation . . . ?" (Heb. 2:3). There is nothing more that God can do.

Death does not change us—it fixes us. Some argue that "the last trump," "the dead in Christ shall rise first," and "we shall all be changed in the twinkling of an eye" refer not so much to the spirit as the body—the soul has other opportunities. But the Holy Spirit says, "Let the . . . filthy still be filthy" (Rev. 22:11, RSV).

When the time comes all that are doing wrong will do it more and more. The vile will become more vile; good men will be better; those who are holy will continue on in greater holiness. But in death the rudder is already set—our direction is already fixed.

How eager God is for us all to make our choice now. It is today that is determining tomorrow. We take with us into the next life what we have made of ourselves in this life.

Some time ago *Presbyterian Life* magazine contained these words:

> Hell is a condition of deadened sensitivity. It would be hell:
>
> to be surrounded by love and not be able to respond;
>
> to live in the midst of great truth and not believe it;
>
> to listen to great music of heaven: harp, trumpet, and chorus and sense nothing of it;
>
> to see matchless beauty of heaven, streets, mansions, trees of life, and be unmoved by it;
>
> to walk through the years with Jesus Christ, moving like a haunting shadow beside us, but to see nothing in him.

How should this doctrine affect us? Everything about our lives should make God attractive to others—our works should woo them, our attitudes should attract them, our love should lead them to his love, our prayers should make them aware of their need for divine strength and authority, and our compassion should compel us to a greater witness.

7
*HEAVEN—
THE FINAL
HOME*

WITHOUT REVELATION, THE LAST BOOK OF the Bible, the story of Christianity ends in partial uncertainty—like a great bridge consisting of only the first arch of the history of God's plan in the past. It seems to be gaping in the air, unsupported by the other span that must come to rest on the solid rock of a certain tomorrow. Without this revelation, our Christian faith is an unfinished story, leaving us with groping uncertainties, with questions and doubts.

The earlier Scriptures informed us of the preexistent Christ, his incarnation, his miracles, his teaching, his agony and death, and his resurrection and ascension into heaven. Before he left us, he made the promise that there were many other things he would tell us but that we could not bear them. The Holy Spirit would reveal them to us. This included his further revelation to us about the things to come. The pages of Revelation claim to be the fulfillment of his promise.

My wife and I were picking flowers on a 10,000-foot mountain, deeply impressed by the majesty of God's handiwork. We took some of the flowers home and placed them in a vase to enjoy their beauty. Others on the mountain had plucked some of the same, brought them into a laboratory, examined them through the microscope, analyzed their structure, fiber, and color, thus gaining a knowledge and inspiration lost to us. This book but picks and mentions some of the figurative flowers, the beautiful symbols and the majestic metaphors talked about. We but point out the presence of these details.

We have visited desert stretches and mountainous areas glancing at and admiring species of rock and stone. Others have put these stones in boxes or bags and taken them to their lapidary shops to cut through them to find their hidden wonders of beauty missed by us. They were able to discover the unpolished jewels which we, in our haste, were missing. But we had been deeply impressed by the sweep of vision and the mountain height on which we had stood. There is just so much to see that we couldn't take it all in.

This book is but a short visit to the great vital experience of tomorrow and a walk through and across those five lofty revelations about death, the intermediate state, the resurrections, the judgments, and heaven, our final home.

Our libraries are richly filled with countless volumes dealing with the various interpretations and meaning of the words and symbols for those who desire further study. We simply mention some of these truths allowing for differences of interpretations to tempt others to a fuller study.

WHAT IS HEAVEN?

The word *ouranos* in Greek usually denotes an "uplifted place." It symbolizes a moral height, and above that it represents the noble rather than the ignoble. It often means "that which is above," something heavenly or celestial rather than earthly or terrestrial. Homer spoke of it as "the sky immediately above us."

To the Hebrews, heaven is spoken of in terms of the layers of sky, but only in a figurative sense. The Hebrew word is *shamayim,* a plural. The heavens are where the trees breathe and rain falls from above. The heavens are where the birds fly. The heavens are also where sun, moon, and stars move in their orbits. The highest heaven was said to be where God dwells in a special way.

Modern science recognizes layers of the heavens, and some of it seems to coincide with earlier ideas. Above ground-level atmosphere, the area from 20 to 30 miles up is called the *stratosphere*. From 30 to 50 miles is called the *mesosphere,* and from 50 to 300 the *ionosphere.* Above that, from 300 to 20,000 miles is called the *exosphere*. Since these categories are not entirely new it helps us to understand that the ancients made some differentiation as well.

In the highest scriptural sense, heaven is the abode of God, his dwelling place—and the final abode of believers. This is not to deny that God is omnipresent. Heaven is a place where God is revealed and understood by his creation—not just a place where he is "contained." Heaven is God's approachable dwelling place, where God shall dwell with men and they shall be his people, "a place for thee to dwell in for ever" (2 Chron. 6:2, RSV).

Some say heaven is located on some distant planet. Certainly it is possible for God to find a planet for the habitation of his people. He would have no difficulty in using one of his millions of planets as a home for the new Jerusalem and the new heaven. Some hold this conjecture as a possibility both scientifically and spiritually.

There is some question about the nature of the new Jerusalem, however, which seems to take place on earth and at a future time period referred to as the millennium, a subject which needs further study and explanation.

WHAT IS THE MILLENNIUM?

This term *millennium* is derived from the combination of two Latin words: *mille,* meaning "thousand," and *annum* meaning "year," denoting a thousand years. Theologically, it refers to the thousand years of perfection, health, happiness, and righteousness spoken of in the Scriptures as the time when Christ will reign on earth.

> Then I saw an angel come down from heaven with the key to the bottomless pit and a heavy chain in his hand. He seized the Dragon—that old Serpent, the devil, Satan—and bound him in chains for 1,000 years, and threw him into the bottomless pit, which he then shut and locked, so that he could not fool the nations any more until the thousand years were finished. Afterwards he would be released again for a little while. Then I saw thrones, and sitting on them were those who had been given the right to judge. And I saw the souls of those who had been beheaded for their testimony about Jesus, for proclaiming the Word of God, and who had not worshiped the Creature or his statue, nor accepted his mark on their foreheads or their hands. They had come to life again and now they reigned with Christ for a thousand years (Rev. 20:1-4, TLB).

There are a number of different interpretations about the millennium among Christians as to when or where the events will take place, and whether or not the reference to a thousand years is literal or figurative.

The *amillennialists* contend that there will be a final reign of Christ in the universe for all time, and the moment one accepts Christ, for them the millennium has begun. They believe that the number of years spoken about is figurative language describing an eternity in heaven.

The *postmillennialists* believe that we are now in the millennium because of the progress the Church has made through the centuries—and that the Church should do all it can to make the world in order for Christ's return. These point to the futility of praying the Lord's prayer, "Thy kingdom come," because they say it has already begun. They believe the Church must be active and establish his kingdom here and be ready for his return and so become happier as this time goes on with the success of the gospel. These feel that the abolition of child labor, slavery, and the growth of Christianity across the world make today a part of the millennium and indicate that Satan is being gradually bound. But the worsening world conditions and two world wars convinced many postmillennialists that Satan was not bound and that the world was not getting better and better but worse and worse.

The *premillennialists* believe that the millennium will begin with the visible return of Christ to take over the reign of government and then under his rule there will be tranquility and peace, when men will beat their swords into plowshares and their spears into pruning hooks. During that thousand years the world will not be burdened with warfare and chaos. Only when Christ comes again will his will be done on earth as it is in heaven.

One comforting thing about these three interpretations is that they all believe in the great consummation of things when Jesus Christ will be on the throne as King of kings and Lord of lords. They only disagree on how and when he takes the throne.

During this thousand years the devil and his forces are to be cast into the pit. Many believers have tried to envision what would happen during that time when the Church of Jesus Christ can go ahead with its program without the interference of the organized forces of satanic evil.

ISRAEL IN THE FUTURE

Paul foretold in Romans that God was not finished with Israel. This nation would return to God, accepting Christ as the Messiah, and would launch a dynamic missionary effort to all civilization as part of the new and eternal Church. Many would look upon him whom "they had pierced," and would claim him as their Messiah.

Note how clearly the Holy Spirit has guided the writers of Holy Scripture to unite these prophecies with one great network, each echoing or complementing the other as they wrote the Gospels, the Epistles, and Revelation (Romans 11). Paul explained that Israel was the original tree of the covenant, but because of disobedience and failure to carry out the will of Jehovah, it had been set aside for awhile and the Gentiles were engrafted into the tree of God's spiritual enterprise and purpose. But God has not forgotten that Israel has a covenant with him. We Gentiles have, in this interval, seen the scattering of the Hebrew nation, and we have been given the burden or privilege of preaching this gospel throughout the world.

But what about Israel today? Israel became a nation in 1948. In 1950 the Knesset passed the proclamation of "The Law of Return." Every Jew could return to

Israel and claim citizenship. Fifty thousand returned from the Yemen, 100,000 returned from Iraq. Later 120,000 more, mostly descendants from the Babylonian captivity. They kept coming from North Africa, 98 percent of the Jews from Libya, 93 percent of the Egyptian Jews, 99 percent of those from Syria, 60 percent of the Jews of Morocco, and 70 percent from Tunisia. Overall, in about the last twenty-five years, Jews have come from 102 nations where they had been living for centuries.

There were several reasons for their return. Some came because of the pogroms that had taken place around the world where efforts had been made to exterminate them as a race. Israel needed manpower and skills to develop its infant nation. It also needed an army capable of defending it on all sides. Such a fighting force was needed in the Six-Day War. The Old Testament prophecied that the Jews would one day return to their promised land in just such numbers.

Two hundred seventy thousand Jews have left Israel in the last thirty years, a conference on emigration reported in 1981. In signing for temporary visas some Israelis buy the return trip tickets required but remain abroad permanently because of an enormous inflation rate, high taxes, low wages, poor employment opportunities, and a six-day work week. In 1981 some secretaries made $60 per week and a doctor about $120. Housing is also poor. The head of government housing said that part of the problem was Israel's materialistic society. In 1981 the government estimated that Israel's Jewish population is 3.3 million, but officials admit that some of the citizens on paper may now be living abroad.

Despite the picture in Israel, one cannot help but see

that God is doing something unusual in that land that ultimately will affect the coming millennium.

WHAT HEAVEN WILL BE LIKE

The size of heaven is significant. "The city lies foursquare, its length the same as its breadth . . . twelve thousand stadia [or about 1,500 miles]" (Rev. 21:16, RSV). F. W. Boreham thought it worthwhile to ask how many the city might accommodate. An Australian engineer named Tammas, one of his parishoners, described it as having an area of 2,250,000 square miles. London has an area of 140 square miles. The city in Revelation is fifteen thousand times as large as London, twenty times as big as New Zealand, even bigger than India—an enormous continent in itself.

How many inhabitants would be possible in such a city? As to population, it is more wonderful still. Working on the basis of the number of people per square mile in London, the population of the city foursquare comes out at about one hundred billion (one followed by eleven zeroes)—seventy times the present population of the world.

What of the occupations of heaven? There will be rest, but it will not be empty loafing. Heaven's eternity will give us the time to meditate on the greatness and goodness of God. It will allow the mind to delve into the fulness of truth denied us in the past fussiness of life.

In heaven we will serve God day and night (Rev. 7:15). Heaven does not mean loafing incessantly. Heaven will permit us alternatives. It will be work without weariness. It will be a joyous job that will be given, a task that will never be tedious. It will not be performed for gain but for the glory of God.

Heavenly service will not be performed for pay but for the praise of God, not for salary but for the smile of the Master's approval. It will be motion with high motives.

Late in his life, Rudyard Kipling penned his hope in these lines:

> *When earth's last picture is painted, and the tubes are twisted and dried,*
> *When the oldest colors have faded, and the youngest critic has died,*
> *We shall rest, and—faith, we shall need it,—lie down for an aeon or two,*
> *Till the Master of all Good Workmen shall set us to work anew!*
>
> *And only the Master shall praise us, and only the Master shall blame;*
> *And no one shall work for money, and no one shall work for fame;*
> *But each for the joy of working, and each in his separate star*
> *Shall draw the Thing as he sees It for the God of the things as They are!*

At a certain church the mission days opened daily with a 6:30 A.M. Bible study hour. The woman who chaired the occasion was doing an excellent job of using only fifteen minutes to serve everyone breakfast, giving us forty-five minutes for unhurried study of the Living Bread. Stepping into the kitchen I praised her for using a "gift" the Holy Spirit had bestowed on her. Rather puzzled she said, "What gift? I'm embarrassed that I have none."

I reminded her of the gift of helps. "Few women could do what you have been doing. The test of any gift is the degree to which it edifies or builds up the church. How you have ministered has helped us all this week. Perhaps you and Martha in the Scriptures will be thanked by the Master as will multitudes of others for the part they played in the total ministry of Christ in the places they were serving."

MUSIC IN HEAVEN

The Creator, it appears in Scripture, loves music and placed the same love in the hearts of his people. Jubal was the "father of all those who play the lyre and pipe" (Gen. 4:21, RSV). The worship of God and the highest ceremonies included the cornet, cymbals, dulcimer, flute, sackbut, viol, and lyre. Eight times trumpets are mentioned as having a part in the unfolding revelation of the New Testament and Revelation. Miriam sang with her timbrel and heartened the women in exile (Ex. 15:20).

There is also singing in heaven. "I saw a Lamb standing on Mount Zion in Jerusalem, and with him . . . this tremendous choir—144,000 strong—sang a wonderful new song in front of the throne of God and before the four Living Beings and the twenty-four Elders" (Rev. 14:1, 3, TLB).

I was once sitting beside an aged cattleman in a large camp meeting. After a hymn he said, "I don't have any trouble carrying a tune—it's unloading it that's so hard." But he knew he would sing in heaven. When Handel, directing his great "Messiah" impatiently called, "Louder, louder!" they knew his plea would be answered up there—someday.

Christ, at the last supper with his disciples, before he went to his cross and death, invited them to join him in a hymn (Mark 14:25, 26). Paul admonished his churches to sing, partly in rehearsal for the songs in heaven and for spiritual vitality here: "Speaking to yourselves in psalms and hymns and spiritual songs, singing and making melody in your heart to the Lord" (Eph. 5:19).

John wrote: "And I heard a voice from heaven, as the voice of many waters . . . and they sung, as it were a new song before the throne" (Rev. 14:2, 3).

The music of heaven! What a field of service for the godly composers of history to write for the glory of God their new songs and orchestrations for the millions that make up that eternal family!

A PLACE PREPARED FOR US

Before we come to the consideration of heaven, the final abode of the righteous, it might be well for us to consider the other places and conditions in which God fellowshiped with humanity—the only creation made in his image.

God is love and love naturally wants an object on which to bestow its affection. So God created man and woman in his own likeness, his own image, that he might have fellowship with them, talk with them, work with them.

The place prepared for them is pictured as the Garden of Eden. Rich in verdure, plentiful in fruit, beautiful in every way—it pleased God. Adam and Eve are pictured as pleased with it as well, walking with God, talking with him, in close and unbroken fellowship. There is one limitation placed upon them—they were not to eat of a certain tree of knowledge, for in doing so they would set out on a road of rebellion that would end in spiritual death. Satan, who was allowed to exist, as God's antagonist, became active. Beguiled by Satan, Adam and Eve defied God and ate of the tree, losing their happy habitation in the garden with God. Their son Cain murdered Abel because of his jealous rebellion. This was the result of the seeds their parents had sown in their own rebellion against God.

Noah and his family followed Jehovah, but the inhabitants of the land became lawless. God then sent the flood to cleanse the scene again to make fellowship with his people easier.

As we examine these efforts of God to have a place of fellowship with his creation, we better understand part of God's purpose in heaven. Jesus said, "I go to prepare a place for you" (John 14:2).

ANGELS IN HEAVEN

Angels are a part of the many things that God has prepared for them that love him. Many times angels have been a part of God's program and their past becomes inseparably connected with their future. They will be doing in the future what they are now doing and have been doing in the past.

Angels are a special free-willed creation of God. Since that rebellion against Jehovah as described in Ezekiel 28, Satan and his demons have tried all manner of means to create chaos, heartache, rebellion, and confusion in human history.

There is scarcely a religious era or system, ancient or modern, that has not been cursed by the malevolences of these organized beings surrounding the prince of devils, Satan. We are promised much of the same in the future until these evil angels are cast into outer darkness in God's good time.

The Scriptures tell some of what the angels say and do. They act as go-betweens for heaven and this world. They announced Christ's birth, and were present to aid him in his various ministries while in the flesh.

Karl Barth, the well-known theologian, took his solid stance as to his convictions concerning the existence of angels in his book *Doctrine of Creation*. He said, "It is true, of course, that we can miss the angels. We can deny them altogether. We can dismiss them as superfluous or absurd and comic. We can protest with frowning brow and clenched fist that, although we might admit there is a God, it is going too far to allow that there are angels as well. . . . If we cannot . . . accept angels, how can we accept what is told us by the history of Scripture or the history of the church or of the history of the Jews, or of our own life's history? . . . Where God is, there the angels of God are. Where there are no angels there is no God."

THE MINISTRY OF ANGELS TODAY

I have been enjoying several volumes in which people in our own times have been confident of God's promise, "He shall give his angels charge over thee to keep thee in all thy ways" (Ps. 91:11).

Through the centuries and in the present, many have noted a very conscious presence of protection guarding them against their enemies; armed men have stopped in terror, feeling they have been opposed by unseen forces. Missionaries have told of extraordinary deliverances from dangers. His "holy ones" seem to be active in the here and now. Mobs threatening groups of believers have been stopped in their tracks. Demon-possessed attackers have been shocked into immobility and a dynamic light has appeared to block their vengeance. Many have claimed actual manifestations of angels.

The Scriptures give us ample confidence as to the angels' temporal and military might in the last days. "When the Son of man comes in his glory, and all the angels with him, then he will sit on his glorious throne" (Matt. 25:31, RSV). This heavenly host that had on other occasions assured God's people of victory will guarantee his total reign in the climax of history.

For sentimental reasons some have erroneously felt that their children who died became little angels. But angels are entirely different forms of creation. When we, born a "little lower than angels," accept Christ, we become through the new birth, the children of God, an honor the angels do not enjoy. In this sense, Christians become a little higher than the angels as the Scriptures never refer to angels as children of God.

WE WILL KNOW LOVED ONES IN HEAVEN
I think we shall know our loved ones and countless others besides. We use words such as "loved ones" usually in a limited sense as denoting certain human ties, such as husband and wife. Paul wrote concerning marriage and the future: "If the husband be dead, she [the wife] is loosed from the law of her husband . . . she is no adulteress, though she be married to another man" (Rom. 7:2, 3). Death severs the marriage bond. Personal affection is probably not carried into our hea-

venly state. Think of those who would weep and mourn if the loving mate had not made it to the kingdom or if they all had! What tears those absences or presences would create!

I did say, however, with a smile to my wife, that even if I had an equal affection for all God's people up there, she should not be surprised when I made it to heaven, if I sought her out and walked with her a bit longer than with any other woman. She smiled. How earthly and mortal we are! But perhaps the Father might understand my earthiness and he might smile also.

If parental love were there, what heartache and crying would ensue if all parents and their children had not met the requirements of eternal life! Many believe, as I do, that the joys of heaven are so broad and all-encompassing that our love for all the righteous will be sufficient to make and keep our joys complete.

The love of God is no respecter of persons and Scripture has taught us that, "As many as received him, to them gave he power to become the sons of God" (John 1:12). In calling God, "Father," Christ becomes our elder brother and all Christians in the world become our brothers and sisters in Jesus Christ. Thus he has made us all members of the same household of faith, each spiritually belonging to the other.

Our deeper love for each other has not decreased; our celestial love has increased to take in the myriads of those who love him.

WE WILL SEE GOD FACE TO FACE
No man could see the full majesty and light of God without being affected. Moses, when he came down

from the mountain, knew not that "his skin shone because he had been talking with God." Jacob said in surprise: "I have seen God face to face, and yet my life is preserved" (Gen. 32:30). Paul wrote: "Now we see in a mirror [glass] dimly, but then face to face" (1 Cor. 13:12, RSV). The sun in its brilliance is seen only through protective glasses. Even in a time of its eclipse we must see it only through a dark glass or a very small aperture.

But fuller sight and knowledge of God is promised us in heaven. Years ago we enjoyed the story gleaned from the *Westminister Teacher* about an artist's daughter who had lost her eyesight when she was a baby. After her mother died, the girl's father became her constant and affectionate companion. For years her blindness was considered incurable. Then a new type of surgery promised to restore her vision. Following the operation as she lay in a darkened room with bandaged eyes, this one thought occupied her mind. Soon she would see her father. When the days of waiting had passed, the dressings were removed, and at last she looked into the compassionate face she had so long desired to see. Trembling with excitement, she closed her eyes and then opened them again to convince herself she was not dreaming. As the one she loved took her in his arms, she exclaimed, "I've had such a good-looking father all these years and didn't even know it!"

The experience of this girl made me think of the beautiful promise of Revelation 22:4, "And they shall see his face." Although the inhibiting bandages of our mortal limitations still block from our view the delightful vision of God's face, we have this present aid: that when man, by searching, sophistry, and philosophy, could not find God, it pleased God to reveal himself.

We agreed at the beginning of this book that the Holy Spirit might not answer enough of our questions regarding our future to satisfy our curiosity, but he would tell us enough to quiet and allay our concerns. The fears of what might await us are calmed by the fact of who awaits us.

John Baillie, noted British theologian and scholar told of a man who had been informed by his doctor that his end was near. He asked the doctor if he had any convictions as to what awaited him in the beyond. He fumbled for an answer. Before he could speak there was a scratching at the door; and his answer was given him. The man said, "Do you hear that? That is my dog. I left him downstairs but he grew impatient and has come up and hears my voice. He has no notion what is inside this room but he knows that I am here. Now is it not the same with us? We do not know what is beyond that door, but we know the Master is there."

WE SHALL SEE CHRIST
It was always Christ's wish, the passion that led to his pain and death on the cross, to be with those who believed in him. He had been in the beginning with the Father, enjoying the worship of heaven, the thrill of the throne and yet was willing to empty himself and take on the form of a servant and become obedient unto death on the cross—for us.

His great desire was, "Father, I would that they be with me in the glory." What a love—how stunningly unselfish a goal for a king.

I mentioned earlier how I as a boy of eleven heard my sister in her last minute of this life of fourteen years say, "Jesus is holding my hand." Just a year or so later my mother had the privilege of leading to Christ, in our hometown jail, a man who had been termed by the press as a "man without a soul." He had been in jail most of the thirty-two years of his life. He had been convicted of murder. He had changed the hymn "We shall see the King someday," to "I shall see the King Friday," the day he was to be hanged.

Word came that a woman appeared whose testimony could free the condemned man, but he chose rather to go ahead with the execution, so ready was he to see the Lord. Weary of bars and trials he perferred to "go home." His white shirt was left open at the collar to allow for the rope. The last words I heard were his song, "I shall see the King today." And I believe he did.

One of the most endearing hymns today is "How Great Thou Art." Its triumphant ending in the last stanza breathes the same high desire, the greatest longing and expectation:

> *When Christ shall come with shout of acclamation*
> *And take me home, what joy shall fill my heart!*
> *Then I shall bow in humble adoration*
> *And there proclaim, "My God, how great Thou art."*
> *Then sings my soul, My Saviour God to Thee:*
> *"How great Thou art! How great Thou art!"*
>
> [Stuard E. Hine]